Bibliotheca Indo-Buddhica S

VIPASSANĀ :
A Universal Buddhist Meditation Technique

Edited by

D.C. Ahir

Sri Satguru Publications

A Division of

Indian Books Centre

Delhi - India

Published by :
Sri Satguru Publications
A Division of
Indian Books Centre
Indological and Oriental Publishers
40/5, Shakti Nagar,
Delhi-110007
(INDIA)

ISBN 81-7030-612-4

First Edition : Delhi, 1999

Published by Sunil Gupta for Sri Satguru Publications a division of
Indian Books Centre, 40/5, Shakti Nagar, Delhi-110 007, India and
printed at Mudran Bharti, Delhi-110007

Preface

Ever since I turned to Buddhism I had been interested in Meditation. Therefore, the very first article I contributed to the Maha Bodhi journal of the Maha Bodhi Society of India, Calcutta, in February 1960, was on "Meditation In Buddhism". But that understanding of Buddhist Meditation was at theoritical level. How to meditate in a systmatic manner and how to attain self-mastery over mind I learnt many years later when I joined a Vipassanā Course at Jaipur in November 1986. It so happened that after my retirement from Government service in February 1986, my wife and I visited England to meet our elder son, Nirmal Kumar, living there. It was at Luton in England on 24 August 1986 that, through the courtesy of my friend Gurmukh Sidhu, I first of all heard a Talk on Vipassanā by Acharya S.N. Goenka, who also happened to be on a visit to U.K. at that time. Inspired by this talk, the first thing I did on return to India was to join the first available ten-day course (No. 278) at Jaipur in November 1986. During the course, I per chance came to know about the forthcoming Seminar On Vipassanā Meditation to be held at Dhammagiri, Igatpuri (Maharashtra) from 20 December 1986 to Ist January 1987. I immediately applied for permission to participate in this Seminar. On being permitted, I not only participated in this 15-day Seminar-cum-Course (No. 280) but also presented a scholarly paper on "Vipassanā and Asoka's Dhamma". Thus from November 1986 onward, I am closely associated with the Vipassana movement in India.

The primary object of this book is to highlight the universal character of Vipassanā, a Buddhist Meditation Technique, a meditation which can be practised by any one in the world without any distinction of colour, creed, race or religion. The study begins with a brief historical background of the advent of Vipassana in modern India, and its growing popularity in all parts of the world. It is followed by eight essays by the modern teachers of Vipassanā on the theory and practice of this unique meditation. Then there is a scholarly analysis of 'Silence : Its Reach And Spiritual Significance' followed by a study of 'Vipassanā And Asoka's Dhamma', and 'Place of Jhana And Samadhi in Theravada Buddhism'. The next six essays bring out in bold relief the benefits of Vipassanā Meditation to individuals and society. And to make this study complete in all respects, the Code of Discipline to be followed during a Vipassanā Course, and the Satipatthana Sutta, the Discourse on the Foundations of this Unique Meditation Technique, have also been added.

I am greatly indebited to the authors and publishers of the material included in this volume on Vipassanā Meditation.

Buddha Jayanti
May 11, 1998

D.C. Ahir

Contents

1
Introduction

The Advent Of Vipassanā In Modern India

Vipassanā is the most ancient meditation technique of India. It was discovered by Gautama the Buddha more than 2,500 years ago at the time of His Supreme Enlightenment at Bodh Gaya. The most important discourse ever given by the Buddha on Vipassanā meditation or mental development is the Satipatthana Sutta, No. 10 in Majjhima Nikaya. There is also a Maha Satipatthana Sutta which appears at S.No. 22 of Digha Nikaya. Both these discourses were delivered by the Buddha when He was staying at Kammasadamma, a market town in the Kuru country, near Delhi, the capital of modern India.

For about 1000 years, Vipassanā floruished in India. However, when Buddhism declined in India. Vipassanā also vanished leaving no trace whatsoever. Luckily, it was preserved in its pristine purity in the neighbouring country of Burma (Myanmar) by the Burmese Bhikkhu-Sangha in the teacher-pupil tradition through the ages. The two foremost Vipassanā Mediation teachers in modern Myanmar were the Venerable Ledi Sayadaw and the Venerabale Mahasi Sayadaw.

Till the beginning of the 20th century, the Vipassana meditation masters were only the venerable monks. The first lay Vipassanā teacher was a farmer Saya Thetgyi (1873-1945), a disciple of Ven. Ledi Sayadaw, with whom he stayed for seven years learning and perfecting the meditation technique. It was in 1915 that U Thet taught Vipassanā for the first time to a group of about

25 monks, well-versed in the scriptures, and residing in the monastery of Ledi Sayadaw. From then onward, he came to be known as Saya Thetgyi (*saya* means "teacher" and *gyi* is a suffix denoting respect).

Returning to his village, Saya Thetgyi started conducting regular Vipassanā courses in his village, Pyawbwegyi. Soon his reputation as a meditation teacher spread. He taught simple farmers and labourers, as well as those who were well-versed in the Pali texts. Since his village was not far off from Rangoon, the capital of Burma, a number of government employees and city dwellers also came. One of them was U Ba Khin, who turned out to be the greatest exponent of Vipassanā meditation in modern times.

Sayagyi U Ba Khin was born in Rangoon on 6 March, 1899. In 1917, he passed the high school examination, and joined Government service in the office of the Accountant General of Burma.

In 1937, U Ba Khin joined the first Vipassanā ten day course under Saya Thetgyi; he progressed well and continued the practice during his frequent visits to Saya Thetgyi's Centre. U Ba Khin became Accountant General on 4 January 1948, the day Burma gained independence. For the next two decades he was employed in various capacities in the government, most of the time holding two or more posts, each equivalent to the head of a department. U Ba Khin combined his responsibilities and talents as a government official with his strong Dhamma volition to help spread the teaching of the Buddha. In 1952, he established the International Meditation Centre (I.M.C.), two miles north of the famous Shwedagon Pagoda in Rangoon. Here many Burmese and foreign students had the good fortune to learn Vipassanā technique from Sayagyi U Ba Khin. Sayagyi finally retired from government service in 1967, and from that time until his death in January 1971 he stayed at the International Meditation Centre teaching Vipassana.

Sayagyi U Ba Khin was keen that the Vipassanā Meditation should go back to India, its original home, and from there spread afar. He was himself very eager to come to India to teach Vipassanā to Indian people. But he was unable to do so as at that time it was extremely difficult for a Burmese citizen to get a passport for foreign travel.

Since, however, Vipassanā was destined to come back to India, Satya Narayan Goenka, an Indian born in 1924 in Burma (now known as Myanmar) became its vehicle. Goenka had joined a Vipassanā Course under Sayagyi U Ba Khin for the first time in 1955. For the next 14 years, he took training under U Ba Khin, and was named as 'teacher' by his illustrious Master. Sayagyi was keen that the Vipassanā should go back to India, and help the suffering humanity in the land of its birth. S.N. Goenka took this as the mission of his life and leaving behind his flourishing business in Burma, he came back to India in 1969 with the Vipassanā technique as his proud posssession. So this unique meditation technique was handed down by the Venerable Ledi Sayadaw to Saya Thetgyi, by Saya Thetgyi to Sayagyi U Ba Khin, and by Sayagyi U Ba Khin to S.N. Goenka, who brought back the precious gem to India, its original home.

The story of Goenka's first encounter with Vipassanā; his training under Sayagyi U Ba Khin, and re-introduction of Vipassana meditation in India can better be described in Goenkaji's own words. He says:

"It was in 1954, my physicians in Burma advised me to get myself treated in foreign countries; otherwise there was a danger of my becoming a morphine addict. I was suffering from a severe type of migraine since my childhood, the intensity and frequency of which had increased with years. Even the best doctor in Burma had no treatment for it except that he administered morphine injection whenever I suffered from an attack which came about every fortnight. This was certainly not a treatment. That is why they warned me that there was a danger of my starting to crave for morphine; not because of this headache, but because of my gradual addiction to it.

On their advice, I made a trip round the world and for months together was under the treatment of some of the best doctors in Switzerland, Germany, England, United States and Japan. But it was all in vain. It proved a sheer waste of time, money, and energy, I returned no better.

At this stage, my good friend (Kalyan Mitta) U Chan Htoon, who later became a judge of the Supreme Court of the Union of Burma and President of the World Fellowship of Buddhists, guided me to Sayagyi U Ba Khin. I shall always remain grateful to him and shall keep on sharing with him all the merits that I accumulate while treading this Noble Path.

My first meeting with this saintly person, U Ba Khin, had a great impact on me. I felt a great attraction towards him and the peace which emanated from his entire being. I straight away promised him that I shall be attending one of his ten-day intensive Vipassanā meditation courses in the near future. In spite of this promise I kept on wavering and hesitating for the next six months, partly because of my skepticism about the efficacy of meditation in curing my migraine which the best available medicine in the world could not do, and partly because of my own misgivings about Buddhism, having been born and brought up in a staunch, orthodox and conservative Sanatani Hindu family. I had a wrong notion that Buddhism was a pure nivriti marg, a path of renunciation and had no real hope for those who were not prepared to renounce the world. And I was certainly not prepared to do so at the prime of my youth.

In spite of these hesitations, there was something deep within me which kept on pushing me towards that great saint; towards Vipassana Centre at Inyamyaing, the Island of Peace, and towards that Noble Path with which I must have had past acquaintance although I was unaware of the same then. Hence, after the monsoon was over, when the Meditation courses were resumed at the centre, I participated for ten days.

These were the most illuminating days of my life. The migraine had proved a blessing in disguise. A new Goenka was born. A second birth was experienced in coming out of the shell of ignorance. It was a major turning point in my life. Now I was on the straight path of Dhamma without any blind alleys from which one had to retreat one's steps. I was on the royal road to real peace and happiness, to liberation and emancipation from all sufferings and miseries.

All the doubts and misgivings were gone. The physical suffering of migraine was so trivial compared to the huge mass of invisible suffering in which I was involved. Hence a relief from migraine was a mere by-product. The self-introspection by Vipassana had shown me that my whole being was nothing but a mass of knots and Gordian knots of tensions, intrigues, malice, hatred, jealousy, ill-will, etc. Now I realized my real suffering. Now I realized that deep rooted, real causes of my suffering. And here I was with a remedy that could totally eradicate these causes, resulting in the complete cure of the suffering itself. Here I was with a wonderful detergent which could clean all the stains of my dirty psychic Linen. Here I was with a hitherto unknown simple technique which was capable of untying all those Gordian knots which I had kept on tying up ignorantly in the past resulting in an all time tension and suffering.

Walking on this path, using this detergent, taking this medicine, practising this simple technique of Vipassana, I started enjoying the beneficial results, here and now, in this very life. The *Sanditthiko* and *Akaliko* qualities of Dhamma started manifesting themselves and they were really fascinating to me, for like my teacher, I too had been a practical man all my life, giving all the importance to the present.

Now I was established on the path from which there was no looking back but a constant march ahead. Not only my migraine was totally cured, but all my misgivings about the Dhamma were also gone. I fully understood that a monk's renounced life was certainly preferable to achieve the goal with the least hindrance, but the householder's life was not an insurmountable barrier to the achievement. Millions upon millions of house-holders in the past and present have benefited from this Eight-fold Noble Path which is equally good for the monks as well as the householders, which is equally beneficial to young and old, men and women; verily, to all human beings belonging to any caste, class, community, country, profession, or language group. There are no narrow sectarian limitations in the path. It is universal, it is for all human beings for all times and all places.

It was my great *punna-parmi* indeed, that I was born and brought up in Burma, the land of living Dhamma; that I came in contact with Sayagyi U Ba Khin, the saintly exponent of the Noble

Path; that I could avail of his compassionate guidance and proximity, to practise the Saddhamma continuously for 14 years; that now I find myself in an unexpected opportunity wherein I can gratefully serve my teacher in fulfilling his lifelong cherished desire to spread the applied Dhamma to the suffering humanity so that more and more people at large can get Shanti-Sukha, the peace and harmony that they badly need.

While in Burma I had the privilege of sitting at his pious feet and translating his words into Hindi language for his Indian students for about 10 years. It was indeed a sacred opportunity for me to have remained so near to him and near to his inifinite Metta waves. Then it so happened that I received a message from my mother in Bombay that she was ill and when her condition deteriorated she started calling me to come to see her.

The Revolutionary Government of Burma was kind enough to grant me the necessary passport valid for a visit and stay in India for a period of 5 years. Hence in June 1969, I came to Bombay, and with the blessings of Sayagyi, I conducted the first course of Vipassana meditation for the benefit of my mother, wherein 13 others participated, some known and others unknown to me. At the conclusion of the course my mother was greatly relieved of her illness and other participants were also immensely benefited. On repeated requests from these participants and to serve further my old ailing mother, I conducted a few more courses with the blessings of Sayagyi and then the ball started rolling. Receiving requests from different parts of India I kept on moving and conducting course after course from place to place where not only local residents but people from different parts of the world started participating. All these courses were conducted under personal guidance and blessing of my teacher. Even after his passing away, observing the continued success of these courses, I get more and more convinced that it is his *Metta* force which is giving me all the inspiration and strength to serve so many people from different countries. Obviously the force of Dhamma is immeasurable."

This is the story in brief of the advent of the Vipassana Meditation in modern India by Kalyanmitta S.N. Goenka. In order to give concrete shape to the wishes of his illustrious teacher, he set up in 1971 a trust known as "U Ba Khin Memorial Trust" to spread Vipassanā in India. Soon the search began for a suitable site for the first Vipassana Centre in the land of the Buddha. Finally, such a site was identified, and a 20-acre hill-top, at Igatpuri, about 140 km from Bombay, on the Bombay-Nasik Road was purchased. The auspicious hill-top was named as "Dhammagiri", "the Hill of Dhamma", and the Vipassana International Academy was established there in 1976.

For learning Vipassanā Meditation it is necessary to undergo a residential course of 10 days' duration. During this period, the students take the vow to follow the five precepts - abstention from killing, stealing, lying, sex and intoxicants. They also take the vow of silence, and are not to communicate with each other in any way or with the outside world for the next 10 days. Even eye contact is discouraged. Reading and writing too is forbidden. In all, the students are required to meditate from 4.30 A.M. to 9.30 P.M. with adequate rest for food and rest.

Notwithstanding such rigid rules and regulations, the code of conduct, and the time table, the Vipassana has become popular rapidly in India and abroad. Apart from its benefits, probably what appeals to people from all religions, and what makes it different is the fact that it relies on no mantras, chants, or even focussing the mind on a particular image. All these are forbidden in Vipassana. No wonder the Vipassana Light which emanated from the Hill of Dhamma (Dhammagiri) has since engulfed the entire world.

The Vipassana International Academy, founded by S.N. Goenka in 1976, has now as many as many 24 Vipassana Centres in India, where atleast one 10-day course is held every month. The Vipassana courses are also conducted at many other places from time to time for the benefit of the local people. The growing popularity of Vipassanā meditation in India may be judged from the fact that in 1995 as many as 27,500 students participated in 350 ten-day and old student courses; 9,500 students participated in 160 children courses, including ten courses for 400 street children; and 33 courses were held in prisons, one of them for children of the inmates.

The spread of Vipassanā in other countries of the world is also phenomenal. The Vipassana International Academy at Dhammagiri, Igatpuri was established in 1976, by the pioneer Indian Vipassana Teacher of modern times. Just within 22 years (1976 - 1998), Vipassana is now quietly sweeping across over 90 countries as diverse as U.S.A., Russia, Cuba, Iran, Israel, Mongolia, Japan as a single-most potent force for individual salvation as well as social change. Vipassana courses are now being conducted for schools, colleges, prisons, management trainees, police officials, bureaucrates, the visually handicapped, and street children.

Encouraged by the world-wide response to Vipassana, and in order to bring this blissful technique within the reach of more and more people, the Vipassana International Academy, in association with the World Vipassana Foundation, has embarked on a big project, erection of a 325 feet high golden pagoda, near Mumbai (Bombay). The fondation stone of this Grand Pagoda was laid on 26 October 1997. The Pagoda will have a hollow interior holding a circular gallery exhibiting the life of the Buddha on His Teachings of Sila (Morality), Samadhi (Meditation) and Panna (Wisdom), and will have a mammoth hall where 10,000 Vipassana students can meditate together around the enshrined Holy Relics of the Buddha.

D.C. Ahir

2
An Exposition Of
Vipassanā Meditation*

Venerable Dr. U Rewata Dhamma

Vipassana means to see things as they really are, not only as they seem to be. The technique of Vipassana is based on the *Satipatthana* Sutta. *Satipatthana* means the establishing of mindfulness. This is one of the oldest and most original teachings of the Buddha and through it one can cultivate mindfulness and develop awareness. The proper practice and application of Vipassana meditation enables one to solve many problems and for this reason it has become a subject of interest and study for Western psychologists. This, however, is not the final goal. If one uses Vipassana Meditation as a treatment for physical and mental ailments it is similar to using a certain medicine for a particular disease. The particular disease may be cured but one still has to face many other diseases as long as one remains in Samsara. Vipassana meditation, indeed, aims at the total purification of human beings and at the overcoming of sorrow, lamentation, the destruction of grief and suffering and the reaching of the right path and the attainment of the Nibbanic state. One who practises Vipassana meditation with this aim in mind, even before he attains the final goal, can achieve peace of mind, happiness, calmness, relaxation and tranquility and the ability to face life's daily problems and enjoy

* The Young Buddhist 1982,
  A Publication of Singapore Buddha-Yana Organisation, Singapore.
  pp 91-93.

a corresponding greater degree of happiness in this very life here and now.

The Satipatthana Sutta on which Vipassana Meditation is based is the oldest and most authoritative treatise on Meditation among the Buddha's teachings. It has been highly respected and very widely practised for the last twenty-five centuries. It is beneficial for all kinds of individuals and many aspects of the practice can be selected by people to meet the needs of their individual temperaments. Here, I would like to explain briefly the methods of practice most commonly used nowadays. There are four arousings or foundations of mindfulness and they are mindfulness of the body (kayanupassana), mindfulness of feeling (vedananupassana), mindfulness of consciousness (cittanupassana) and mindfulness of mental objects (dhammanupassana). Here, mindfulness of the body includes mindfulness of the breath (anapana), mindfulness of the four postures(iriyapatha), mindfulness of the four kinds of clear comprehension (sampajanna), and mindfulness of the four elements of material qualities (dhatumanisikara).

Anapana Sati

Mindfulness of breath (anapanasati) means awareness of respiration on the incoming and outgoing breaths. In the Sutta it merely says how to arouse mindfulness on the object of meditation, that is "to arouse mindfulness in front." It is not made clear where to focus the attention, hence the yogi may wrongly think he must follow the breath inside. But the Buddha in the Patisambhidamagga said to focus the attention at the nostrils, at the point below the nostrils above the upper lip. "Where the breath is felt to pass in and out", is the precise point where the meditator should focus his attention so that awareness can be developed easily. When one breathes in long or short it is necessary to be aware of it just as it is. Thus the yogi develops awareness of the whole breath. Sometimes a yogi may mistakenly understand this instruction to mean that he has to experience the whole physical body whilst breathing in and out. But the body here means the breath. If one focuses his attention at the nostrils just above the upper lip one can be aware of the incoming and outgoing breath at the nostrils. Generally, the meditator will be aware of the whole breath process at that point, when his awareness and concentration has been developed to some extent. Moreover, his respiration will grow more subtle. At first the breath is gross and coarse but in as much as awareness is developed the breath becomes more and more subtle and a proper and more precise awareness of the breath arises. It is said in the Sutta, "Calming the activity of the body" here the body again refers to the breath. Initially the breath is very strong and gross. In as much as awareness of concentration is developed to that extent does the breath become more calm and subtle. Sometimes, however, the breath is so subtle that the meditattor has difficulty in being aware of the breath at all and consequently may feel as if the breath has disappeared or ceased.

The Four Postures and Elements

Mindfulness of the four postures refers to awareness of the four modes of walking, sitting, standing and lying, when they occur. The four kinds of clear comprehension means awareness in going forwards, in going backwards, looking straight on and looking away. It includes awareness of the processes of walking, sitting, standing and lying, and awareness of all other physical activities too. It means that awareness should be developed in detail and maintained from moment to moment. Clear comprehension here, means the discerning of things rightly, entirely equally.

Mindfulness of the four elements of material qualities means to be aware of the four elements of which the body is composed. If one gives bare attention to the body one can experience heaviness and lightness, cohesion, heat and cold (temperature) and motion in the body. Then one can develop awareness of these four elements.

Feelings

Mindfulness of feelings is as follows. There are many kinds of sensations in the body and they are both gross and subtle in type. They can be divided into two categories, namely, bodily feelings (*kayikavedana*) and mental feelings (*cetasika-vedana*).

Bodily feelings are of three kinds, pleasure (*sukkha*) pain (*dukkha*) and neither pleasure nor pain (*adukkha-asukkha*). Mental feelings are also of three types, joy (*somanassa*), grief (*domanassa*) and neither joy nor grief (*upekkha*). Whatever feelings we experience we have to maintain a precise moment to moment awareness of them. All kinds of feelings, physical or mental, gross or subtle, are included in the term *vedana*. It is essential to develop a precise awareness whenever any of these feelings arise, in as much as concentration and awareness are developed that much is one able to develop awareness of the gross and subtle feelings and will experience them as they are and be able to note the arising of them from moment to moment.

Consciousness

Mindfulness of consciousness is mentioned in the Satipatthana Sutta and there it says that when consciousness arises with lust, hate and with delusion etc. one should be aware at the very moment when they arise. It is however difficult for the meditator to be aware of these types of consciousness all the time as these particular types of consciousness do not arise all the time. The best way to practise the mindfulness of consciousness is as follows: When, for example, the eye and visible object meet and seeing arises, one is to be aware of the seeing consciousness. In the same way, one is to be aware when hearing, smelling, tasting and touching. When consciousness arises at the sense bases, it is important to know that awareness itself, is consciousness. When this awareness arises it is important to be aware of that awareness. For example, when one is watching the imcoming and outgoing breaths one is to be aware not only of the incoming and outgoing breaths but also one must note one's being aware of one's awareness of the breath going in and out. In this way, one can practise awarenss of consciousness from moment to moment.

All Kinds of Mental Objects

Mindfulness of mental objects refers to all kinds of mental and material objects, because of which consciousness arises. The

Sutta names many different kinds of mental objects such as the five hindrances (*nirvaranas*) – passion, ill-will, sloth and torpor, agitation, worry and doubt; the five aggregates of clinging (*upadanakhandha*) – material form, feeling, perception, formations and consciousness; the six external and internal bases (*ayatana*) – eye, ear, nose, tongue, body and mind; sight, sound, odour, taste, tangible objects and mental objects; the seven factors of Enlightenment (*bojjhanga*) mindfulness, investigation, effort, joy, calmness, concentration, and equanimity; and the four truths – suffering, the cause of suffering, the cessation of suffering and the path leading to the cessation of suffering. These mental objects are nothing more than human experience in a mundane or supramundane state, and therefore all Vipassana meditation technique is based on the four arousings of mindfulness. According to tradition whoever starts to practise meditation has to begin with the meditation on the body and the feelings, because mindfulness of consciousness and mental objects is so subtle that it is difficult for beginners to be aware of them. When they start to practise mindfulness of breathing after a few days' practice as much as awareness and concentration is developed, to that extent is one able to be aware of the subtle sensations, consciousness (*awareness*) and mental objects. There are four aspects of practice for the development of awareness and concentration. They are: *Anativattanattha*, meaning that the object and awareness of the object should arise together and precisely. Second is *Ekarasattha*, meaning the function of the senses and the mind must be the same; for example, when one sees an object the first moment of seeing is just seeing, there is no sign, shape or form etc. seeing is reality (*paramattha*); this is the object of the seeing sense. In the same way, mind will accept seeing as seeing without any labelling. Therefore when seeing, hearing, feeling, thinking, etc., arise one is to be aware just of the seeing, hearing, thinking etc. *Viriyavahanattha* is the third aspect and it is right effort in the sense of persistence, and is the means by which the object and awareness arise together. *Asevanattha*, the fourth aspect means continual practice. The aforesaid three conditions will function properly when one practises again and again. If one follows these four aspects of practice properly, one will be able to experience the arising and passing away of the objects from moment to moment, and realise that whatever physical or mental processes arise, all are subject to change and none of them remain the same for two consecutive moments. Moreover, because of this impermance (*anicca*) there is unsatisfactoriness (*dukkha*) and there is no permanent *substance* in any of these processes that can be called I or self (*atta*). Experience of these three characteristics of things is called Vipassana or Insight, seeing things as they really are and only as they seem to be. At that moment the meditator will acquire an ability to accept things (*nama-rupa*) without concept or notion (*pannatti*) and can overcome like and dislike for them and remain with just the awareness of those processes. The Buddha wanted us to understand *annica* by direct experience. If one understands *anicca* perfectly one understands *dukkha* as its sequel and realises *anatta* in its ultimate sense. This is the purpose of practising Vipassana Meditation.

Three Kinds of Profound Knowledge

One who practises Vipassanā properly will then gradually acquire three kinds of profound knowledge, namely, autological knowledge, analytical knowledge and dispelling knowledge. At first the meditator realises the characteristics of the mental and physical processes with their proximate causes. This means that the meditator comes to know that this is materiality whilst that is mentality and also breath-awareness etc. This stage of realistation is called *autological knowledge*. After this stage comes the understanding called *analytical knowledge* in which the meditator will realise the three characteristics.

After this stage the meditator will eliminate the concept of permanence and happiness (*nicca-sukkha and sukkha-sanna*) and this stage is called dispelling knowledge. On the other hand, the meditator does realise at the *autological stage* the characteristic of each mental and physical phenomenon he experiences. At the *analytical stage* he realises the common characteristics of (*anicca*) impermanence, (*dukkha*) suffering and (*anatta*) non-self. *At the dispelling stage* he will eliminate all hallucinations, the concept of permanence together with concepts of happiness and self.

These profound knowledges belong to the mundane world and include all stages of insight (*vipassana*). Anyone who acquires these stages of profound knowledge will come to experience the path (*magga*) and its fruition (*phala*) and experience the Nibbanic peace within and enjoy the fruits of that Path.

3
On The Path
(Training At The Centre)*

Sayagyi U Ba Khin

Whoever is desirous of undergoing a course of training in Vipassanā Meditaion must go along the Noble Eightfold Path. This Noble Eightfold Path was laid down by the Buddha in his first sermon to the five ascetics (Pañca-vaggiyā) as the means to the end, and all the student has to do is to follow strictly and diligently the three steps of *Sīla, Sam*ādhi and *Paññā*, which form the essence of the Noble Eightfold Path.

Sīla (The Precepts)

1. Right Speech
2. Right Action
3. Right Livelihood.

   Samādhi (Equanimity of Mind)

4. Right Exertion
5. Right Attentiveness
6. Right Concentration

   Paññā (Wisdom, Insight)

7. Right Aspiration
8. Right Understanding

---

* The article is an extract of the paper read by Sayagyi U Ba Khin, to the press representatives of Israel on the 12th December, 1961, at the International Meditation Centre, Rangoon, on the occasion of the visit of their Prime Minister Mr. Ben Gurion to Burma.

Sīla

For the first step, *sīla,* the student will have to maintain a minimum standard of morality by way of a promise to refrain from killing sentient beings, stealing others' property, committing sexual misconduct, telling lies and taking intoxicating drinks. This promise is not, I believe, detrimental to any religious faith.

Samādhi

This is the second step, the development of the power of concentration to the degree of one-pointedness of mind. It is a way of training the mind to become tranquil, pure, and strong, and therefore forms the essence of religious life, whether one be a Buddhist, a Jew, a Christian, a Hindu, a Muslim or a Sikh. It is, in fact, the greatest common denominator of all religions. Unless one can get the mind freed from impurities (*Nīvaraṇa*) and develop it to a state of purity, he can hardly identify himself with Brahma or God. Although different methods are used by people of different religions, the goal for the development of mind is the same, that is to say, a perfect state of physical and mental calm.

The student at the Centre is helped to develop the power of concentration to one-pointedness by encouraging him to focus his attention on a spot on the upper lip at the base of the nose, synchronizing the inward and outward motion of respiration with the silent awareness of in-breath and out-breath. Whether the energy of life is from mental forces (*Saṅkhārā*) resulting from one's own actions, as in Buddhism, or from God, as in Christianity, the symbol of life is the same. It is the rhythm, pulsation, or vibration latent in man. Respiration is, in fact, a reflection of this symbol of life. In the *'Anāpāna* meditation technique (i.e., respiration mindfulness) which is followed at the Centre, one great advantage is that the respiration is not only natural, but is also available at all times for the purpose of anchoring one's attention to it, to the exclusion of all other thoughts. With a determined effort to narrow down the range of thought waves, first to the area around the nose with respiration mindfulness and gradually, with the wave-length of respiration becoming shorter and shorter, to a spot on the upper lip with just the warmth of the breath, there is no reason why a good student in meditation should not be able to secure one-pointedness of mind in a few days of training.

There are always *pointers* to the progress of this meditation when steered in the right direction, by way of symbols which take the form of something "white" as opposed to anything "black". They are in the form of clouds or cotton wool, and sometimes in shapes of white such as smoke or cobwebs or a flower of disc. But when the attention becomes more concentrated, they appear as flashes or points of light or as a tiny star or moon or sun. If these pointers appear in meditation (with the eyes closed, of course), then it should be taken for granted that *Samādhi* is being established. What is essential, then, is for the student to try after each short spell of relaxation to get back to *Samādhi* with the pointer of "light" as quickly as possible. If he can do this, he is quite ready to be switched on to Vipassanā meditation to gain insight into the Ultimate Truth and enjoy the Great Peace of *Nibbāna*. If he is able to focus his attention *on one point* at the base of the nose with *a minute point* remaining stationary for some time it is all the better, because at that time he reaches *Upacāra Samādhi* or Neighbourhood concentration.

"Mind is intrinsically pure," the Buddha said, "It becomes polluted however, by the absorption of impurities *(Akusala* forces)." In the same way meditation can eventually get his mind distilled of impurities and brought to a perfect state of purity.

Paññā

Paññā means insight into what is true of nature which is realized only when one has attained the Noble Paths (*Magga*) and enjoyed the fruits (*Phala*) of his endeavours in Buddhist Meditation. Meditation is inseparable from the development of the power of mind towards *Samādhi* and the intimate study of what is true of nature towards the realization of the truth.

When the student has reached a certain level of *Samādhi*, preferably *Upacāra Samādhi*, the course of training is changed to Vipassana or Insight. This requires the use of the powerful lens of

Samadhi already developed and involves an examination of the inherent tendencies of all that exists within one's own self. He is taught to become sensitive to the on-going processes of his own organism which, in other words, are sub-atomic reactions ever taking place in all living beings. When the student becomes engrossed in such sensations, which are the products of nature, he comes to the realization, physically and mentally, of the Truth that his whole physical being is after all a changing mass. This is the fundamental concept of *Anicca* in Buddhism – the nature of the change that is ever taking place in everything, whether animate or inanimate, that exists in this universe. The corollary is the concept of *Dukkha* - the innate nature of suffering or ill – which becomes identified with life. This is true because of the fact that the whole structure of a being is made up of sub-atomic particles (*Kalāpas* in Buddhism), all in a state of perpetual combustion. The last concept is that of *Anattā*. You call a substance whatever appears to you to be a substance. In reality there is no substance as such. As the course of meditation progresses, the student comes to the realization that there is no substantiality in his so-called self, and there is no such thing as the core of a being. Eventually he breaks down the ego-centralism in himself – both in respect to mind and body. He then emerges out of meditation with a new out-look – ego-less and selfless – alive to the fact that whatever happens in this Universe is subject to the fundamental laws of cause and effect. He knows with his inward eye the illusory nature of the separate self.

The Fruits of Meditation

The Fruits of Meditation are innumerable. They are embodied in the discourse on the advantages of a *Samana's* life, the *Samañña-phala Sutta*. The very object of becoming a *Samana* or monk is to follow strictly and diligently the Noble Eightfold Path and enjoy not only the Fruition (*Phala*) of *Sotāpatti, Sakadāgāmi* and *Anāgāmi* and *Arahatta,* but also to develop many kinds of faculties. A layman who takes to meditation to gain insight into the Ultimate Truth also has to work in the same way, and if his potentials are good, he may also enjoy a share of those fruits and faculties.

Only those who take to meditation with good intentions can be assured of success. With the development of the purity and power of the mind, backed by insight into the Ultimate Truth of nature, one might be able to do a lot of things in the right direction for the benefit of mankind.

The Buddha said, "O monks, develop the power of concentration. He who is developed in the power of concentration sees things in their true perspective."

This is true of a person who is developed in *Samādhi*. It must be all the more so in the case of a person who is developed not only in *Samādhi* but also in *Paññā* (Insight).

It is a common belief that a man whose power of concentration is good and who can secure a perfect balance of mind at will can achieve better results than a person who is not so developed. There are, therefore, definitely many advantages that accrue to a person who undergoes a successful course of training in meditation, whether he be a religious man, an administrator, a politician, a businessman or a student.

4

The Art Of Living : Vipassanā Meditation

S.N. Goenka

Everyone seeks peace and harmony, because these are what we lack in our lives. From time to time we all experience agitation, irritation, disharmony, suffering; and when one suffers from agitation, one does not keep this misery limited to oneself. One keeps distributing it to others as well. The agitation permeates the atmosphere around the miserable person. Everyone else who comes into contact with him becomes irritated, agitated. Certainly this is not the right way to live.

One ought to live at peace with oneself, and at peace with all others. After all, a human being is a social being. He has to live in society—to live and deal with others. How to live peacefully? How to remain harmonius within ourselves and to maintain peace and harmony around us, so that others also can live peacefully and harmoniously?

When one is agitated, then, to come out of it, one has to know the basic reason for the agitation, the cause of the suffering. If one investigates the problem, it soon becomes clear that whenever one starts generating any negativity or defilement in the mind, one is bound to become agitated. A negativity in the mind, a mental defilement or impurity, cannot co-exist with peace and harmony.

---

* This article is based on a public talk given by S.N. Goenka in Bern, Switzerland on 16 July, 1980.

How does one start generating negativity? Again investigating, it becomes clear. I become very unhappy when I find someone behaving in a way which I don't like, when I find something happening which I don't like. Unwanted things happen and I create tension within myself. Wanted things do not happen, some obstacles come in the way, and again I create tension within myself; I start tying knots within myself. Throughout the life, unwanted things keep on happening, wanted things may or may not happen, and this process of reaction, of tying knots–Gordian knots–makes the entire mental and physical structure so tense, so full of negativity. Life becomes miserable.

Now one way to solve the problem is to arrange that nothing unwanted happens in my life, and that everything keeps on happening exactly as I desire. I must develop such power, or somebody else must have the power and must come to my aid when I request him, that nothing unwanted happens in my life and that everything I want should keep on happening. But this is not possible. There is no one in the world whose desires are always fulfilled, in whose life everything happens according to his wishes, without anything unwished-for happening. Things keep on occurring that are contrary to our desires and wishes. Then, in spite of these things which I don't like, how not to react blindly? How not to create tension? How to remain peaceful and harmonious?

In India as well as in other countries, wise saintly persons of the past studied this problem – the problem of human suffering – and they found a solution: if something unwanted happens and one starts to react by generating anger, fear or any negativity, then as soon as possible one should divert one's attention to something else. For example, get up, take a glass of water, start drinking – your anger will not multiply and you'll be coming out of anger. Or start counting: one, two, three, four. Or start repreating a word, or a phrase, or perhaps some mantra – it becomes easy if you use the name of a deity or saintly person to whom you have devotion; the mind is diverted, and to some extent you'll be out of the negativity, out of anger.

This solution was helpful; it worked. It still works. Practising this, the mind feels free from agitation. In fact, however, the solution works only at the conscious level. Actually, by diverting the attention, one pushes the negativity deep into the unconscious, and on this level one continues to generate and multiply the same defilement. At the surface level there is a layer of peace and harmony, but in the depths of the mind is a sleeping volcano of suppressed negativity which keeps on exploding in violent eruption from time to time.

Other explorers of inner truth went still further in their search; and by experiencing the reality of mind and matter within themselves they recognized that diverting the attention is only running away from the problem. Escape is no solution; one must face the problem. Whenever a negativity arises in the mind, just observe it, face it. As soon as one starts observing any mental defilement, then it begins to lose all its strength. Slowly it withers away and is uprooted.

A good solution, avoiding both extremes of suppression and of free license. Keeping the negativity in the unconscious will not eradicate it; and allowing it to manifest in physical or vocal action will only create more problems. If one just observes, then the defilement passes away, and one has eradicated that negativity, is freed from that defilement.

This sounds wonderful, but is it really practical? When anger arises, it overpowers us so quickly that we don't even notice. Then, overpowered by anger, we commit certain actions physically or vocally which are harmful to us and to others. Later, when the anger has passed, we start crying and repenting, begging pardon from this or that person or God: "Oh, I made a mistake, please excuse me!" Again the next time, in a similar situation, we react in the same way. All that repenting does not help at all.

The difficulty is that I am not aware when a defilement starts. It begins deep at the unconscious level of the mind, and by the time it reaches the conscious level, it has gained so much strength that it overwhelmes me and I cannot observe it.

Then I must keep a private secretary with me, so that whenever anger starts, he says, "Look master, anger is starting!" since I don't know when this anger will start, I must have three private secretaries for three shifts, around the clock; or, rather, four of them to give staggering holidays!

Suppose I can afford that, and the anger starts to arise. At once my secretary tells me, "Oh, master, look–anger has started!" Then the first thing I do is slap and abuse him: "You fool! Do you think you are paid to teach me?" I am so overpowered by anger that no good advice will help.

Even supposing wisdom prevails and I do not slap him. Instead I say, "Thank you very much. Now I must sit down and observe anger." Yet is it possible? As soon as I close my eyes and try to observe the anger, immediately the object of anger comes into the mind–the person or incident because of which I became angry. Then I am not observing the anger. Rather, I am observing the external stimulus of the emotion. This will only multiply the anger; this is no solution. It is very difficult to observe any abstract negativity, abstract emotion, divorced from the external object which aroused it.

However, one who reached the ultimate truth in full enlightenment found a real solution. He discovered that whenever any defilement arises in the mind, two things simultaneously start happening at the physical level. One is that the breath loses its normal rhythm. I start breathing hard whenever a negativity comes into the mind. This is one reality which everyone can experience, though it may be very gross and apparent. Also, at a subtler level, some kind of biochemical reaction starts within the body – some sensation. Every defilement will generate one sensation or the other inside, in one part or another of the body.

This is a practical solution. An ordinary person cannot observe abstract defilements of the mind, abstract fear, anger, or passion. But with proper training and practice, it is very easy to observe the respiration and the sensations both of which are directly related to the mental defilement.

The respiration and sensations will help me in two ways. Firstly, they will be my private secretaries. As soon as a defilement starts in the mind, my breath will lose its normality; it will start shouting: "Look, something has gone wrong!" I cannot slap the breath; I have to accept the warning. Similarly the sensations tell me: "Something has gone wrong." I must accept it. Then, having been warned, I start observing the respiration, the sensations, and I find very quickly that the defilement passes away.

This mental-physical phenomenon is like a coin with two sides. On the one side is whatever thoughts or emotions arising in the mind. On the other side are the respiration and sensation in the body. Any thought or emotion, whether conscious or unconscious any mental defilement manifests in the breath and sensation of that moment. Thus, by observing the respiration or the sensation, I am indirectly observing the mental defilement. Instead of running away from the problem, I am facing the reality as it is. Then I shall find that the defilement loses its strength; it can no longer overpower me as it did in the past. If I persist, the defilement eventually disappears altogether; and I remain peaceful and happy.

In this way, the technique of self-observation shows us reality in its two aspects, inner and outer. Previously, one always looked with open eyes, missing the inner truth I always looked outside for the cause of my unhappiness; I always blamed and tried to change the reality outside. Being ignorant of the inner reality. I never understood that the cause of suffering lies within, in my own blind reactions.

It is difficult to observe the abstract negativity when it arises; but now, by training, I can see the other side of the coin: I can be aware of the breathing and also of what is happening inside me. Whatever it is, the breath or any sensation. I learn just to observe it, without losing the balance of the mind. I stop multiplying my miseries. Instead, I allow the defilement to manifest and pass away.

The more one practises this technique, the more he will find how quickly he can come out of the negativity. Gradually the mind becomes freed of the defilments; it becomes pure. A pure mind is always full of love – disinterested love for all others; full of compassion for the failings and suffering of others; full of joy at their success and happiness; full of equanimity in the face of any situation.

When one reaches this stage, then the entire pattern of one's life starts changing. It is no longer possible for one to do anything vocally or physically which will disturb the peace and happiness of others. Instead, the balanced mind not only becomes peaceful in itself, but it helps others also to become peaceful. The atmosphere surrounding such a person will become permeated with peace and harmony, and this will start affecting others, too.

This is what the Buddha taught: an art of living. He never established or taught any religion, any "ism." He never instructed followers to practise any rites or rituals, any blind or empty formalities. Instead, he taught just to observe nature as it is, by observing the reality inside. Out of ignorance, one keeps reacting in a way which is harmful to oneself and to others.

Then when wisdom arises – the wisdom of observing the reality as it is – one comes out of this habit of reaction. When one ceases to react blindly, then one is capable of real action – action proceeding from a balanced, equanimous mind, a mind which sees and understands the truth. Such action can only be positive, creative, helpful to oneself and to others.

What is necessary, then, is to know thyself – advice which every wise person has given. One must know oneself not just at the intellectual level, at the level of ideas and theories. Nor does this mean to know at the devotional or emotional level, simply accepting blindly what one has heard or read. Such knowledge is not enough.

Rather, one must know reality at the actual level. One must experience directly the reality of this mental-physical phenomenon. This alone is what will help us come out of defilements, out of sufferings.

This direct experience of one's own reality, this technique of self-observation, is what is called "Vipassana" meditation. In the language of India in the time of the Buddha, passanā meant to look, to see with open eyes, in the ordinary way; but Vipassanā is to observe things as they really are, not just as they seem to be. Apparent truth has to be penetrated, until one reaches the ultimate truth of the entire mental and physical structure. When one experiences this truth, then one learns to stop reacting blindly, to stop creating defilements–and naturally the old defilements gradually are eradicated. One comes out of all miseries, and experiences happiness.

There are three steps to the training which is given in a meditation course. Firstly, one must abstain from any action, physical or vocal, which disturbs the peace and harmony of others. One cannot work to liberate oneself from defilements in the mind while at the same time one continues to perform deeds of body and speech which only multiply those defilements. Therefore, a code of morality is the essential first step of the practice. One undertakes not to kill, not to steal, not to commit sexual misconduct, not to speak lies, and not to use intoxicants. By abstaining from such actions, one allows the mind to quiet down.

The next step is to develop some mastery over this wild mind, by training it to remain fixed on a single object: the breath. One tries to keep one's attention for as long as possible on the respiration. This is not a breathing exercise; one does not regulate the breath. Instead one observes the natural respiration as it is, as it comes in, as it goes out. In this way one further calms the mind, so that it is no longer overpowered by violent negativities. At the same time, one is concentrating the mind, making it sharp and penetrating, capable of the work of insight.

These first two steps of living a moral life and controlling the mind are very necessary and beneficial in themselves; but they will lead to self – repression, unless one takes the third step: purifying the mind of defilements by developing insight into one's own nature. This reality, is Vipassana: experiencing one's own reality, by the systemetic and dispassionate observation of the ever – changing mind – matter phenomenon manifesting itself as sensations within oneself. This is the culmination of the teaching of the Buddha: self-purification by self – observation.

This can be practised by one and all. The disease is not sectarian; therefore, the remedy cannot be sectarian, it must be universal. Everyone faces the problem of suffering. When one suffers from anger, it is not Buddhist anger, Hindu anger, or Christian anger; anger is anger. Due to anger, when one becomes agitated, it is not a Christian agitation, or Hindu, or Buddhist. The malady is universal. The remedy must also be universal.

Vipassana is such a remedy. No one will object to a code of living which respects the peace and harmony of others. No one will object to developing control of the mind. No one will object to developing insight into one's own reality, by which it is possible to free the mind of negativities. It is a universal path. It is not a cult. It is not a dogma. It is not a blind faith.

Observing the reality as it is, by observing the truth inside – this is knowing oneself at the actual, experiental level. As one practises, one keeps coming out of the misery of defilements. From the gross, external apparent truth, one penetrates to the ultimate truth of mind and matter. Then one transcends that, and experiences a truth which is beyond mind and matter, beyond time and space, beyond the conditioned field of relativity: the truth of total liberation from all defilements, all impurities, all suffering. Whatever name one gives this ultimate truth, is irrelevant; it is the final goal of everyone.

May you all experience this ultimate truth. May all people come out of their defilements, their misery.' May they enjoy real happiness, real peace, real harmony.

5
Vipassanā Kammatthana

Venerable Dr. Rastrapal Mahathera

The word Vipassana is a compounding of the prefix, upasagga 'Vi' used as the proposition and the root word 'Passana' from verb 'Passati', to see. The pre-fixes are generally used to modify or to add emphasis to the sense of the root words. Here the pre-fix has been applied to carry the vigour of Insight, Clarity, Distinctness, Accuracy, Rightfulness or Specification etc., to the Act of Seeing or Perceiving. Thus the *word 'Vipassana'. as a whole, may be rightfully explained as 'to see or to perceive' correctly and accurately or to go Positive into the Insightness.'* Insightness of what? and what to be perceived or to be seen? It is the Insight or discerning of all the material and mental phenomena or the happenings of the living beings with Rightful Thought and the Rightful Understanding. In other words, *Vipassana Bhavana stands for the "Insight system of Meditation".* By Insight, one should mean, the clear and correct perception of the true nature of things i.e., as they really are. *In other-wise, the Insight means understanding of the Reality itself, that is, the conditioning and the unconditioning of the material phenomena.*

In meditation, control and concentration of the mind for particular object, are considered essential. But in Vipassana, concentration of the mind is found to be a necessity to some extent only. And this is not the ultimate aim of Vipassana. *Vipassana being*

---

* A Guide To The Mind Purification (Vipassana) by Ven. Dr. Rastrapal Mahathera, President, International Meditation Centre, Buddha Gaya, India.

the 'introvert' or the insight system of practising, it directs the thoughts and the activities within oneself, and, therefore, is basically related to the meditator himself. In this process, the mind of the meditator dwelling in equanimity, every moment of the mind arising out of its coming and going, is required to be noticed and observed with full awareness.

In this system, mind remains undisturbed and not supposed to be felt boring. The Truth becomes responsive through direct experience. Due to intensive and continuous observations of every function, action and perception of the body and the mind, namely, 'standing, walking, sitting, lying, touching, seeing, hearing, rising, falling, breathing etc', the knowledge of Insight automatically becomes a reality, and the Mind transforms in the state of Serene, Peace and Happiness. In Vipassana, the objects of meditation, therefore, are the moment to moment position of the Body and the Sensations, Feelings and Thoughts of the Mind, instantly originating by virtue of interactions between the body and the mind. In other words, it is the awareness about the impulses emanating from the material and the mental phenomena.

‘ In the Vipassana method, there being no particular object on which one should keep his mind fixed, ignoring all other sense-organs, namely, eye, ear, nose, tongue and body, the mediator shall have to mind with full awareness every aspect of their movements. He must not allow his Mind to wander away without the least degree of Watchfulness.

Essentialities Needed

It is essential that the meditator should prepare himself for the task before starting with the meditation. The first thing necessary, is to develop a strong Will-Power or Stern Determination. The Fragile Mind tends to be easily tempted, and therefore, will not serve the purpose of reaching the destination. Siddhartha Gautama, the Prince, at the time of his search for Truth, is stated to have spent long six years of penance fruitlessly. By practising rigorous self-mortifications barely living on a single grain of rice, leaves and the roots, even reducing the quantity of food material to nothing, due to utter paucity of nourishment he was reduced to mere skeleton. And came nearer to the death's very door. The narration herein has been inserted without taking into account the tribulations he had to undergo during his boundless previous lives. Having been disgusted with the then prevailing practices of extreme self-mortification and sensual pleasures he decided to maintain the Middle Path and his assertion of attaining the Buddhahood being found certain, he took the under mentioned firm resolution *"Let my body be dried up, the flesh and the sinews be dissoloved, I shall never move from this seat under the Bodhi-Tree, unless I attain the long-cherished Enlightenment, the Buddhahood."* The aspirant after the meditation, therefore, giving up all worldly thoughts and clingings, as practicable, during the course of Vipassana, should possess mental firmness of tireless effort, persistent resolution and unflagging devotion for completion of the practice, in search of the Truth and attainment of the Wisdom in accordance with the Buddha's Teachings or the instructions given by the meditation teachers.

The basic foundations of the meditation, particularly of the Insight system of Meditation, the Vipassana, are considered to be 'Sila' 'Samadhi' and 'Panna'. Sila means Morality, Samadhi means Concentration and Panna means Wisdom. By virtue of developing these three ground-base ingradients through meditation the meditator can be able to remove all the attachment and the fetters for deliverance from the cycle of birth, decay, death and rebirth.

Very Purpose of Vipassana

The purpose of Vipassana meditation or the exercise of Insight, is to analyse the following salient characteristics and may also be explained as the contemplation of Impermanence (Anicca), Unsatisfactoriness (Dukkha) and Non-self (Anatta). The illusory 'Soul' (Atta) or the imaginary 'Self' 'I' theory is very deep-rooted in every living being. The meditator must be aware of this fact, that One-pointedness of the Mind should not be the sole object of Vipassana. In *meditation, repeated recollection of thoughts and feelings or "Anussatis", or the Mindfulness or Awareness falls within the category of the "Samatha". But the "Anupassana" which means, the minutest knowledte of arising and vanishing of the Body and the Mental Phenomena, amounts to the 'Vipassana'. There lies the basic difference between the 'Samatha' and the 'Vipassana.'* After the attainment of Jhanic states or the states of Absorption, the meditator must complete continuously the sensations of 'seeing, hearing, smelling, tasting, touching, knowing etc', clearly, as they arise from any of the six sense-doors, namely, eye, ear, nose, tongue, body and mind. The constant process will bring distinct perception, that the body and the mind are two separate things, only joined together. It will also be perceived, that the object and the mind which directly knows the object, rise and pass away at the very moment of contemplation. Through Insight and Positive understanding the meditator will automatically come to know, that in the mere process of rising, falling and passing away, there exists no permanency, no reliability or enduring entity or soul. *Nowhere exists "me" or "mine".* Everything is impermanent, full of ills or sorrows and soul-less, Thus, through Right Understanding and the full development of factual knowledge of 'Anicca, Dukkha and Anatta' there arises the Insight of the Path (Magga) and the Fruition (Phala). That is, entering into the stream of awareness of the moment to moment all the sensations and the results thereof attained or perceived. This is the realization of the Nibbana or the eradication of all worldly attachments and fetters of cause and effect, the sources of lust, hatred and delusion or otherwise, the bondages of birth, decay, death and rebirth. Thus one becomes the Sovereign Monarch of the State of All Blissfulness, Joy and Eternal Happiness. *One must keep in Mind, that contemplating on the Body, Feelings, Consciousness and the Mind-objects, that is, all Anupassanas together,* in other words, as proclaimed by the Buddha, *Samudaya Dhammanupassana, Vayadhammanupassana and Samudaya Vayadhammanupassana only constitute the stages of the Vipassana and thereby, the meditator can free himself, otherwise not.*

6
Vipassanā Meditation :
A Practical Method

William Hart

The teaching of the Buddha is a system for developing self-knowledge as a means to self-transformation. For such a purpose, mere book-learning or erudition will not suffice, being only borrowed knowledge, the acceptance of what others have discovered, not one's own insight. Nor is the knowledge gained by intellectual investigation sufficient, since it is an understanding only at the theoretical level. Both these types of knowledge are helpful only if they lead to *bhāvanā-maya paññā*, the understanding which arises from direct experience of the truth or more precisely, the insight arising from the practice of meditation. With an experiential understanding, we can eliminate the misapprehensions which cause us to act wrongly and to make ourselves unhappy. Instead we learn to act in accordance with reality, and therefore to lead productive, useful, happy lives.

In the *Satipaṭṭhāna Sutta*; the Buddha presented a practical method to develop self-knowledge through self-observation. This technique is Vipassana meditation.

Anyone who tries to observe the truth about oneself' has two aspects, physical and psychic, body and mind. We must learn to

---

* The Maha Bodhi, Volume 93, July-September 1985, pp. 126-30
  William Hart is the author of the "*The Art of Living – Vipassana Meditation As Taught*" -By S.N. Goenka, Vipassana Research Institute, Dhammagiri, Igatpuri, 1987.

observe both. But how actually to experience the reality of body and mind? Accepting the explanations of others is not sufficient, nor is depending on merely intellectual knowledge. Both may guide as in the work of self-exploration but each of us must explore and experience reality directly attain ourselves.

We each experience the reality of the body by feeling it, by means of the physical sensations which arise within it. With eyes closed we know that we have hands, or any of the other parts of the body because we can feel them. As a book has external form and internal content, the physical structure has an external objective reality...the body (kāya) .. and an internal, subjective reality sensation (vedanā). We digest a book by reading all the words in it; we experience the body by feeling sensations. Without awareness of sensation there can be no direct knowledge of the physical structure. The two are inseparable.

Similarly the psychic structure can be analyzed into form and content : the mind (citta) and whatever arises in the mind (dhamma)...any thought, emotion, memory, hope, fear any mental event. As body and sensation cannot be experienced separately, in the same way one cannot observe the mind apart from the contents of the mind. But mind and matter are also closely interrelated. Whatever occurs in one is reflected in the other. This was a key discovery of the Buddha; as he said, 'Whatever arises in the mind is accompanied by sensation."[1]

Thus a human being has a physical aspect of body (kāya) and sensation (vedanā), and a psychic aspect of mind (citta) and mental contents (dhamma). All four can be experienced by observing vedanā. Observation of sensation offers a means to examine the totality of one's being physical as well as mental.

For this reason the Buddha specially stressed the importance of awareness of vedanā. In the Brahmajāla sutta, one of the most important of his discourses, he said, "The Tathagata has become liberated and freed from all attachments by seeing as they really are, the arising and passing away of sensations, the relishing of them, the danger of them, the release from them.[2] Awareness of vedana he stated, is a prerequisite for the understanding of the four

Noble Truths : To whomever experiences sensation I show the way to realize what is suffering, what is its origin, what is its cessation, and what is the path leading to its cessation."[3]

The question then arises, what exactly is *vedanā*? The Buddha described it in various ways. He included *vedanā* among the four aggregates or processes which compose the mind (*khandhā*). However when defining it more Precisely, he spoke of not only mental but physical *vedanā*.[4] In broad terms, *vedana* is obviously a phenomenon having both mental and physical aspects. Matter alone cannot feed anything if mind is not present; in a dead body, for example, there are no sensations. It is the mind that feels, but what it feels has a physical base. Whatever we encounter in life throught the five physical senses and through the mind manifests as sensation within the body. If we do not give attention to what happens in the body, then we remain unaware of the sensation. In the darkness of ignorance a reaction begins toward the sensation, a momentary liking or disliking, which develops into craving or aversion. The unconscious reaction is repeated and intensified innumerable times before it impinges on the conscious mind. If a meditator gives importance only to what happens in the mind, then he becomes aware of the process after the reaction has occurred and gathered dangerous strength, sufficient to overwhelm him. He allows the spark of sensation to ignite a raging fire before trying to extinguish it. He needlessly makes difficulties for himself. But if he learns to observe sensations within the body objectively, then he permits each spark to burn itself out without starting a conflagration. By giving importance to the physical aspect, he becomes aware of *vedanā* as soon as it arises, and can prevent any reaction of craving or aversion from occurring.

The physical aspect of *vedanā* is particularly important because it offers vivid, tangible experience of the reality of impermanence within oneself. *Anicca* is a fact to be observed not just in the external world over a more or less prolonged span of time. Change occurs at every moment within the mental-physical structure, manifesting in the play of sensations within the body. It is at this level that imremanence must be experienced. Observation of the constantly changing sensations permits the realization of one's own ephemeral nature. With this direct experience of *anicca*, one can not only avert fresh reactions of craving or aversion, but can eliminate the very habit of reacting. In this way one gradually frees the mind of suffering.

Unless its physical aspect is included, the awareness of *vedanā* remains partial and incomplete. If based on such a superficial awareness, the understanding of impermanence will be intellectual rather than experiential. Such a superficial understanding is not sufficient to remove the conditionings of craving and aversion rooted in the unconscious mind. So long as these roots remain, the mind is not free from suffering. Therefore the Buddha repeatedly emphasized the importance of the physical aspect for a meditator, in order to gain experiential understanding of the mental-physical structure in its entirety. He said.

Those who continually make efforts

to direct their awareness toward the body,

who abstain from unwholesome actions

and strive to do what should be done,

such people, aware, with full understanding

are freed from their defilements.[5]

The cause of suffering is *tanhā*, craving and its reverse image of aversion. Ordinarily it appears to us that we generate reactions of craving or aversion toward the various objects that we encounter through the physical senses and the mind. The Buddha, however, discovered that between the object and the reaction stands a missing link : *vedanā*. We react not to the exterior reality but to the sensations within us. When we learn to observe sensation without reacting in craving or aversion, the cause of suffering does not arise, and suffering ceases. Therefore observation of *vedanā* is essential in order to practise what the Buddha taught. And the observation must be at the level of physical sensation if the awareness of *vedanā* is to be complete. With the awareness of physical sensation, the meditator can penetrate to the root of the problem and eradicate it. In this way one can observe one's nature to the depths and can liberate oneself from suffering.

Understanding the central importance of the observation of sensation in the teaching of the Buddha, one can gain fresh insight into the *Satipaṭṭhāna Sutta*, "The Discourse on the Establishing of Awareness."

The *sutta* begins by stating the aims of establishing awareness: the purification of beings; the transcending of sorrow and lamentation; the extinguishing of physical and mental suffering; the practising of a way of truth; the direct experience of the ultimate reality, *nibbāna*.[6]

It then briefly explains how to achieve these goals:

Here a meditator dwells ardent with thorough understanding and awareness, observing the body in the body itself, observing sensations in sensations themselves, observing the mind in the mind itself, observing the contents of the mind in the contents of the mind themselves, having abandoned craving and aversion toward the world.[7]

The question at once arises, what is meant by observing body in the body, sensations in sensations, and so forth? For a Vipassana meditator the expression is luminous in the clarity. One must not rely on the explanations of anyone else about one's body or mind, must not view them by one's body or mind, must not view them by one's own preconceptions, nor remain satisfied with a merely intellectual understanding of them. Each of us must experience the reality of ourselves directly. The way to do this, as we have seen, is through observing the sensations within the body. By doing so, one comes face to face with one's own physical and mental nature.

To achieve this direct experience, the meditator must develop two qualities; awareness (*sati*) and thorough understanding (*sampajañña*). The discourse is called "The Establishing of Awareness," but awarenss is incomplete without understanding, insight into the depths of one's own nature, into the impermanence of the entire mental-physical structure. The practice of *satipaṭṭhāna* must bring the meditator to realize for himself the ephemeral nature of his body and mind. When one has had this personal realization, then his awareness is firmly established, right awareness, leading to liberation. Then automatically his craving and aversion disappear not just toward the external world but toward himself the microcosm, the world within. This is where the craving and aversion are most deep-seated, and most often overlooked : in the unthinking attachment toward one's own body and mind. So long as the underlying attachment remains, one cannot be liberated from suffering.

The discourse first discusses observation of the body, *kāyānupassanā*. This is the most apparent aspect of the mental-physical structure, and therefore the proper point from which to begin the work of observation. From this starting point observation of sensations, of mind, and of mental contents naturally develop. Several ways are explained to initiate the observation of body. Of these the first, and most commonly practised, is awareness of respiration. Another way is the giving attention to bodily movements. But no matter how one starts the journey, there are certain stages through which one must pass on the way to the final goal. These are described in a paragraph which is repeated at the end of each section and of each division within a section of the discourse:

> In this way he dwells observing the body in the body internally or externally or both internally and externally. He dwells observing the phenomenon of arising in the body. He dwells observing the phenomenon of passing away in the body. He dwells observing the phenomenon of arising and passing away in the body. Now the awareness presents itself to him, 'This is the ultimate reality of the body.' This awareness develops to such an extent that only understanding and observation remain, and he dwells detached, without clinging to anything in the world.[8] [The word "body" is replaced by "sensations", "mind", and "mental contents" in later sections.]

However he may begin, the meditator must proceed to awareness of sensations in order to experience the reality of the mental-physical structure. He observes the sensations arising in the interior of the body or externally, on the surface of the body, or both together. That is, from awareness of sensations in some parts and not in others, he gradually develops the ability to feel sensations throughout the physical structure. When he begins the practice, he first experiences sensations of a consolidated, perhaps intense nature which arise and seem to persist for some time. He is aware of their arising, and after some time he is aware of their passing away. In this stage he observes the apparent reality of body and mind, their integrated, consolidated, seemingly solid and lasting nature. But as the meditator continues practising, he reaches a stage in which spontaneously the solidity dissolves, and he experiences the mental-physical structure in its true nature as a mass of vibrations, arising and passing away every moment. He realizes the fact of impermanence by experiencing directly the impermanence of himself, moment by moment.

This direct apprehension of the ultimate reality of mind and matter progressively shatters the illusions of the meditator, his misconceptions and preconceptions. Even right conceptions which had been accepted only on faith or by intellectual deduction now acquire new significance when they are experienced. Gradually by the observation of reality within, the mind becomes purified to the point that all the conditionings which distort one's perception are eliminated. Only the faculties of pure awareness and wisdom remain.

As ignorance disappears, the underlying tendencies of craving and aversion are eradicated, and the meditator becomes free from all attachment. Just as ignorance is fundamentally lack of understanding about the reality of oneself, so attachment is fundamentally toward oneself, one's own body and mind. This, the Buddha said, is the real nature of suffering : *pañcupadāna-khandā*, the attachment toward the five aggregates. The world exists for each of us only when we experience it mentally or physically. Ignorance and attachment begin within the microcosm of body and mind. Therefore by developing detachment toward the immediate reality of the mental-physical structure, the meditator develops insight and detachment toward the world. When the attachment is eliminated at its source, then the suffering disappears and one becomes liberated.

The Buddha often said, "whatever is felt is related to suffering."[9] Therefore *vedanā* is an ideal means to explore the truth of suffering. Unpleasnat sensations are obviously suffering, but the most pleasant sensation is also a form of very subtle agitation. Every sensation is impermanent. If one is attached to pleasant sensations, then when they pass away, suffering remains. Thus all sensations contain a seed of *dukkha*.

For this reason, as he spoke of the path leading to the cessation of suffering, the Buddha spoke of two paths proceeding from *vedanā*: that leading to its arising, and that leading to its ceasing.[10] So long as one remains within the sensory field, the conditioned field of mind and matter, sensations and suffering persist. They cease only when one transcends that field to experience the ultimate reality of *nibbāna*.

The Vipassana meditator practises the Noble Eightfold Path by exploring the entire reality of *vedanā* until he reaches the final goal, in which *vedanā* ends. By practising in this way, he experiences directly and vividly all the teaching of the Buddha.

In a verse which has puzzled many translators, the Buddha said.

A man does not really apply Dhamma in life
just because he often speaks about it
But though one might have heard little about it.
if one observes Dhamma by means of his own body
then truly he lives the life of applied Dhamma, and can
never be heedless of the Dhamma.[11]

Our own bodies bear witness to the truth. When a meditator discovers the truth within himself, then it becomes real for him, and he lives according to it. By learning to observe the sensations within ourselves, we can realize that truth, and can attain liberation from suffering.

References

1. Anguttara Nikāya VIII. ix. 3 (83) Mūlaka Sutta. See also Anguttara IX. ii. 4 (14) Samiddhi Sutta.
2. Dīgha Nikāya 1.
3. Anguttara Nikāya III. vii. 61 (ix) Titthāyatana Sutta.
4. Samyutta Nikāya XXXVI. iii. 22 (2) Aṭṭhasata Sutta.
5. Dhammapada XXI. 4 (293).
6. Dīgha Nikaya 22.
7. Ibid.
8. Ibid.
9. Samyutta Nikāya XII. iv. 2 (32) Kalāra Sutta.
10. Samyutta Nikāya XXXVI. iii. 3 (23) Aññatan Bhikkhu Sutta.
11. Dhammapada XIX. 4 (259).

7
The Setting-Up Of Mindfulness*

Ven. Dr. Walpola Rahula Thera,

The most imporatant discourse ever given by the Buddha on mental development (*'Meditation'*) is called the Satipatthana-sutta 'The Setting-up of Mindfulness' (No. 22 of the *Digha-nikaya*, or No. 10 of the *Majjhima-nikaya*). This discourse is so highly venerated in tradition that it is regularly recited not only in Buddhist monasteries, but also in Buddhist homes with members of the family sitting round and listening with deep devotion. Very often *bhikkhus* recite this sutta by the bed-side of a dying man to purify his last thoughts.

The ways of '*meditation*' given in this discourse are not cut off from life, nor do they avoid life; on the contrary, they are all connected with our life, our daily activities, our sorrows and joys, our words and thoughts, our moral and intellectual occupations.

The discourse is divided into four main sections: the first section deals with our body (*kaya*), the second with our feelings and sensations (*vedana*), the third with the mind (*citta*), and the fourth with various moral and intellectual subjects (*Dhamma*).

It should be clearly borne in mind that whatever the form of 'meditation' may be, the essential thing is mindfulness or awareness (*sati*), attention or observation (*anupassana*).

One of the most well-known, popular and practical examples of 'meditation' connected with the body is called 'The Mindfulness or Awareness of in-and-out breathing' (*anapana-sati*). It is for this

---

* The Maha Bodhi, Calcutta, May-June 1973, pp. 165-169.

'meditation' only that a particular and definite posture is prescribed in the text. For other forms of 'meditation, given in this sutta, you may sit, stand, walk, or lie down, as you like. But, for cultivating mindfulness of in-and-out breathing, one should sit, according to the text, 'cross-legged, keeping the body erect and mindfulness alert'. But sitting cross-legged, is not practical and easy for people of all countries, particularly for Westerners. Therefore, those who find it difficult to sit cross-legged, may sit on a chair, 'keeping the body erect and mindfulness alert.' It is very necessary for this exercise that the meditator should sit erect, but not stiff; his hands placed comfortably on his lap. Thus seated, you may close your eyes, or you may gaze at the tip of your nose, as it may be convenient to you.

You breathe in and out all day and night, but you are never mindful of it, you never for a second concentrate your mind on it. Now you are going to do just this. Breathe in and out as usual, without any effort or strain. Now, bring your mind to concentrate on your brathing-in and breathing-out; let your mind watch and observe your breathing in and out; let your mind be aware and vigilant of your breathing in and out. When you breathe, you sometimes take deep breaths, sometimes not, and naturally. This does not matter at all. Breathe normally and naturally. The only thing is that when you take deep breaths you should be aware that they are deep breaths, and so on. In other words, your mind should be so fully concentrated on your breathing that you are aware of its movements and changes. Forget all other things, your surroundings, your environment; do not raise your eyes and look at anything. Try to do this for five or ten minutes.

At the beginning you will find it extremely difficult to bring your mind to concentrate on your breathing. You will be astonished how your mind runs away. It does not stay. You begin to think of various things. You hear sounds outside. Your mind is disturbed and distracted. You may be dismayed and disappointed. But if you continue to practise this exercise twice daily, morning and evening, for about five or ten minutes at a time, you will gradually, by and by, begin to concentrate your mind on your breathing. After a certain period, you will experience just that split second when your mind is fully concentrated on your breathing, when you will not hear even sounds nearby, when no external world exists for you. This slight moment is such a tremendous experience for you, full of joy, happiness and tranquillity, that you would like to continue it. But still you cannot. Yet, if you go on practising this regularly, you may repeat the experience again and again for longer and longer periods. That is the moment when you lose yourself completely in your mindfulness of breathing. As long as you are conscious of yourself you can never concentrate on anything.

This exercise of mindfulness of breathing, which is one of the simplest and easiest practices, is meant to develop concentration leading up to very high mystic attainments (dhyana). Besides, the power of concentration is essential for any kind of deep understanding, penetration, insight into the nature of things, including the realization of Nirvana.

Apart from all this, this exercise on breathing gives you immediate results. It is good for your physical health, for relaxation, sound sleep, and for efficiency in your daily work. It makes you calm and tranquil. Even at moments when you are nervous or excited if you practise this for a couple of minutes, you will see for yourself that you become immediately quiet and at peace. You feel as if you have awakened after a good rest.

Another very important, practical, and useful form of 'meditation' (mental development) is to be aware and mindful to whatever you do, physically or verbally, during the daily routine of work in your life, private, public or professional. Whether you walk, stand, sit, lie down or sleep, whether you stretch or bend your limbs, whether you look around, whether you put on clothes, whether you talk or keep silence, whether you eat or drink, even whether you answer the calls of nature-in these and other activities, you should be fully aware and mindful of the act you perform at the moment. That is to say, that you should live in the present moment, in the present action. This does not mean that you should not think of the past or the future at all. On the contrary you think of them in relation to the present moment, the present action, when and where it is relevant.

People do not generally live in their actions in the present moment. They live in the past or in the future. Though they seem to be doing something now, here, they live somewhere else in their thoughts, in their imaginary problems and worries, usually in the memories of the past or in desires and speculations about the future. Therefore they do not live in, nor do they enjoy, what they do at the moment. So they are unhappy and discontented with the present moment, with the work at hand, and naturally they cannot give themselves fully to what they appear to be doing.

Sometimes you see a man in a restaurant reading while eating—a very common sight. He gives you the impression of being a very busy man, with no time even for eating. You wonder whether he eats or reads. One may say that he does both. In fact, he does neither, he enjoys neither. He is strained, and disturbed in mind, and he does not enjoy what he does at the moment, does not live his life in the present moment, but unconsciously and foolishly tries to escape from life. (This does not mean, however, that one should not talk with a friend while having lunch or dinner).

You cannot escape life however you may try. As long as you live, whether in a town or in a cave, you have to face it and live it. Real life is the present moment—not the memories of the past which is dead and gone, nor the dreams of the future which are not yet born. One who lives in the present moment lives the real life, and he is happiest.

When asked why his disciples, who lived a simple and quiet life with only one meal a day, were so radiant, the Buddha replied: 'They do not repent the past, nor do they brood over the future. They live in the present. Therefore they are radiant. By brooding over the future and repenting the past, fools dry up like green reeds cut down (in the sun).

Mindfulness, or awareness, does not mean that you should think and be conscious 'I am doing this' or 'I am doing that'. No, just the contrary. The moment you think 'I am doing this', you become self-conscious, and then you do not live in the action, but you live in the idea 'I am', and consequently your work too is spoilt. You should forget yourself completely, and lose yourself in what you do. The moment a speaker becomes self-conscious and thinks 'I am addressing an audience', his speech is disturbed and his trend of thought broken. But when he forgets himself in his speech, in his subject, then he is at his best, he speaks well and explains things clearly. All great work–artistic, poetic, intellectual or spiritual–is produced at those moments when its creators are lost completely in their actions, when they forget themselves altogether, and are free from self-consciousness.

The mindfulness or awareness with regard to our activities, taught by the Buddha, is to live in the present moment, to live in the present action. (This is also the Zen way which is based primarily on this teaching). Here in this form of meditation, you haven't got to perform any particular action in order to develop mindfulness, but you have only to be mindful and aware of whatever you may do. You haven't got to spend one second of your precious time on this particular 'meditation': you have only to cultivate mindfulness and awareness always, day and night with regard to all activities in our usual daily life. These two forms of 'meditation' discussed above are connected with our body.

Then there is a way of practising mental development ('meditation') with regard to all our sensations of feelings, whether happy, unhappy or neutral. Let us take only one example. You experience an unhappy, sorrowful sensation. In this state your mind is cloudy, hazy, not clear, it is depressed. In some cases, you do not even see clearly why you have that unhappy feeling. First of all, you should learn not to be unhappy about your unhappy feeling, not to be worried about your worries. But try to see clearly why there is a sensation or a feeling of unhappiness, or worry, or sorrow. Try to examine how it arises, its cause, how it disappears, its cessation. Try to examine it as if you are observing it from outside, without any subjective reaction as a scientist observes some object. Here, too, you should not look at it as 'my feeling' or 'my sensation' subjectively, but only look at it as 'a feeling' or 'a sensation' objectively. You should forget again the false idea of 'I'. when you see its nature, how it arises and disappears, your mind grows dispassionate towards that sensation, and becomes detached and free. It is the same with regard to all sensations or feelings.

Now let us discuss the form of 'meditation' with regard to our-minds. You should be fully aware of the fact whenever your mind is passionate or detached, whenever it is over-powered by hatred, ill-will, jealousy, or is full of love, compassion, whenever it is deluded or has a clear and right understanding, and so on and so forth. We must admit that very often we are afraid or ashamed to look at our own minds. So we prefer to avoid it. One should be bold and sincere and look at one's own mind as one looks at one's face in a mirror.

Here is no attitude of criticising or judging, or discriminating between right and wrong, or good and bad. It is simply observing, watching, examining, You are not a judge, but a scientist. When you observe your mind, and see its true nature clearly, you become dispassionate with regard to its emotions, sentiments and states. Thus you become detached and free, so that you may see things as they are.

Let us take one example. Say you are really angry, overpowered by anger, ill-will, hatred. It is curious, and paradoxical, that the man who is in anger is not really aware, not mindful that he is angry. The moment he becomes aware and mindful of the state of his mind, the moment he sees his anger, it becomes as if it were, shy and ashamed, and begins to subside. You should examine its nature, how it arises, how it disappears. Here again it should be remembered that you should not think 'I am angry', or of 'my anger'. You should only be aware and mindful of the state of an angry mind. You are only observing and examining an angry mind objectively. This should be the attitude with regard to all sentiments, emotions, and states of mind.

Then there is a form of 'meditation' on ethical, spiritual and intellectual subjects. All our studies, reading, discussions, conversation and deliberations on such subjects are included in this 'meditation'. To read this book, and to think deeply about the subjects discussed in it, is a form of meditation.

So, according to this form of meditation, you may study, think, and deliberate on the Five Hindrances (*Nivarana*), namely:

1. lustful desires (*kamacchanda*),
2. ill-will, hatred or anger (*vyapada*),

3. torpor and languor (*thina-middha*),
4. restlessness and worry (*uddhacca-kukkucca*),
5. sceptical doubts (*vicikiccha*).

These five are considred as hindrances to any kind of clear understanding, as a matter of fact, to any kind of progress. When one is over-powered by them and when one does not know how to get rid of them, then one cannot understand right and wrong, or good and bad.

One may also 'meditate' on the Seven Factors of Enlightenment (Bojjhanga). They are:

1. Mindfulness (*sati*), i.e., to be aware and mindful in all activities and movements both physcal and mental, as we discussed above.

2. Investigation and research into the various problems of . doctrine (*dhammavicaya*). Included here are all our religious, ethical and philosophical studies, reading, researches, discussions, conversation, even attending lectures relating to such doctrinal subjects.

3. Energy (*virya*), to work with determination till the end.

4. Joy (*piti*), the quality quite contrary to the pessimistic, gloomy or melancholic attitude of mind.

5. Relaxation (*passaddhi*) of both body and mind. One should not be stiff physically or mentally.

6. Concentration (*samadhi*), as discussed above.

7. Equanimity (*upekkha*), i.e., to be able to face life in all its vicissitudes with calm of mind, tranquillity, without disturbance.

To cultivate these qualities the most essential thing is a genuine wish, will or incination. Many other material and spiritual conditions conducive to the development of each quality are described in the texts.

One may also 'meditate' on such subjects as the Five Aggregates investigating the question 'What is a being' or 'what is it that is called I?', or on the Four Noble Truths, as we discussed above. Study and investigation of these subjects constitutes this fourth form of meditation, which leads to the realization of Ultimate Truth.

Apart from those we have discussed here, there are many other subjects of meditation, traditionally forty in number, among which mention should be made particularly of the four Sublime States: (*Brahma-vihara*): (1) extending unlimited, universal love and good-will (*metta*) to all living beings without any kind of discrimination, 'Just as a mother loves her only child'; (2) compassion (*karuna*) for all living beings who are suffering, in trouble and affliction; (3) sympathetic joy (*mudita*) in others' success, welfare and happiness: and (4) equanimity (*uppekkha*) in all vicissitudes of life.

8
Meditation And Mind Control*

Venerable Acharya Buddharakkhita

Development or degeneration

The role of meditation in effecting the total development of the personality–intellectual, ethical and spiritual, has been beautifully expressed in that famous world-classic, the Dhammapada, in these words:

> Yogā ve jayāti bhūri,
> Ayogā bhurisankhayo;
> Etam dvedha patham ñatva
> Bhavāya vibhāvaya ca,
> Tath'attānam nivseyya
> Yathā bhūri pavad dhati.

–282

"The faculty of intuition which frees one from all bondages, is activated only when the mind is yoked to meditation. This faculty remains Inactive, indeed is even atrophied, when the mind is not cultivated by meditation. There are only two paths, of progress and degeneration. After clearly understanding this, let a man so commit himself that his intuitive wisdom may mature."

This remarkable statement of the Buddha, spells out clearly that there is no third path, no neutralism or 'sitting-on the fence,'

---

* What Meditation Implies, Buddha Vachana Trust, 14 Kalidasa Road, Gandhinagar, Bangalore, Karnataka.

in matters spiritual. You either advance with all vigour or just degenerate. An uncommitted position such as that of the secularist, is untenable and negative. Just as both barrenness and non-cultivation signify unproductivity, so is the uncommitted attitude, barren of positive spiritual results.

Since meditation activates the potential power in man, it has been construed by the Buddha, as the quintessential core of His teachings. The Master uses the picturesque analogy of turning a piece of barren land into a verdant garden to describe what happens to the mind of one who meditates.

Culture of Mind

Meditation is culture of mind. I am using the word 'culture' in the sense it is used in agriculture. That is, cultivating the mind and developing its possibilities to the efflorescence of transcendental perfection. And mind control forms an integral part of the meditative process, even as various control measures form the inevitable operations of agriculture. Mind, said the Buddha, is like a field. If it is kept uncultivated, it remains arid and unproductive, brings forth weeds all through the year causing soil-infertility as also rendering it positively dangerous by harbouring reptiles, scorpions, etc. An analogous situation obtains in the mind. If the mind is not cultivated, not only does it remain unproductive of salutary results, but it brings forth mental weeds in the form of wrong and pernicious thoughts. Greed, hatred and delusion render the mind dangerous.

In contradistinction, when through a systematic culture, the mind is developed, its intrinsic powers are unfolded. And mental culture is not merely an hour or two of actual meditation but a process of development which keeps throughout the waking hours a tempo of inner progress.

In practice, meditation amounts to exercising the mind through a variety of contemplative techniques. Just as by physical culture is meant exercising the body in various ways, even so by mental culture is to be construed a variety of methods whereby the mind is exercised to develop the specifics of mindfulness, concentration and insight. Just as through physical culture one develops strength, overcomes debility, adds to the personality and health, even so through mental culture one overcomes the various mental limitations and weaknesses, builds up positive qualities against evils and temptations, and adds to the layers of spiritual perfections that ultimately occasions freedom from all worldly bondages.

Mind Control

It is to be emphasised that mind control does not mean inhibition of any kind nor does it imply any suppression or repression of natural mental urges. It is essentially a process of self-transcendence. In fact, without a measure of mind control, life will become intractable.

Hence the unambiguous testimony of the Enlightened One:

"Bhikkhus, I know not of any other single thing so unmanageable as the uncontrolled mind. The uncontrolled mind is indeed a thing intractable.

"Bhikkhus, I know not of any other single thing so manageable as the mind controlled. The controlled mind is indeed a thing tractable.

"Bhikkhus, I know not of any other single thing so conducive to great loss as the uncontrolled mind. The untamed mind indeed conduces to great loss.

"Bhikkhus, I know not of any other single thing that brings such misery as the mind that is untamed, uncontrolled, unguarded and unrestrained. Such a mind indeed brings great suffering.

"Bhikkhus, I know not of any other single thing that brings such happiness as the mind that is tamed, controlled, guarded and restrained. Such a mind indeed brings great bliss."

Gradual, not sudden

Self-transcendence results, not so much from an intellectual effort as from a rebirth of the whole personality, *i.e.,* the outlook and attitude, the emotions and the will, and the entire conduct of life. But this total change does not come about, indeed it cannot, all of a sudden. It is a progressive path and a gradual development. Discipline over habits of the body, the change of outlook, the re-patterning of intellectual and volitional activities, and the self-purification resulting from them all, must necessarily be based on a methodology precise and reliable.

Gaṇaka Maudgalyāyana, the famous mathematician of the time, went to the Buddha and asked him, "Venerable Sir, in the case of various avocations, there is always a gradual training, a gradual doing, and a gradual practice. Is it possible, Lord Gotama, to lay down a similar gradual training and a progressive development in respect of the disciplines of spiritual life?"

Methods

Said the Buddha, "It is possible, learned devotee, to lay down a gradual training, in respect of spiritual life. Even as a skilled trainer of horses, trains the horse by getting it used to various modes of training, even so the Tathāgata, the Truth-finder, (i.e., referring to himself in the third person), having taken on a man to be spiritually tamed, disciplines him through a graduated method.

Moral conduct

He is told first, 'Come disciple, be of moral habit through a code of moral purification; live controlled by voluntarily undertaking moral obligations; be endowed with right behaviour and stick to your pasture of morality; see danger in any compromise and defilement of your undertaking; and delight in training yourself in rules of moral conduct.'

Sense control

And as this disciple trains himself this way, the Tathāgata disciplines him further, saying, 'Come, be guarded as to the sense-faculties; be master of your senses. By seeing an object with the eye, do not be entranced by its appearance, but dwell self-controlled. If you do not control your senses, then sensual attractions as also frustrations and other evil states of mind, will flow in. So, fare along, controlling and guarding your senses, the eye, the ear, the nose, the tongue the body, and the mind.'

Moderation in food

And as the disciple fares on, controlling the sense faculties including the mind, he is told, 'Come, be moderate in eating; you should take food reflecting carefully that the purpose of eating is not fun or indulgence or even to get physical charm or beauty but to keep the body going, so that it will assist the spiritual life and enable one to abide in comfort and blamelessness.

Vigilance

The Tathāgata further disciplines him saying' "Now dwell intent on vigilance, cultivate mindfulness and clear comprehension. Turn every action–physical, verbal and mental into a meditational exercise enabling you to remain mindful, clearly alert watching over the body, the feelings, the thoughts and all mental drives and thus cleanse the mind of obstructive mental states."

Overcoming impediments

As soon as the disciple is enabled to remain mindful and discriminative under all situations whether walking or sitting, standing or lying, or doing any work, throughout the waking hours, he is further trained through meditation to have complete control over the mind, thus, "Come now, disciple, train your mind to overcome all thoughts which render the mind uncontrolled. Get rid of the taint of desire and ill-will and dwell generous, benevolent and compassionate. Get rid of laziness and laxity and dwell vigorous, unrelenting, full of energy. Get rid of restlessness and worry and dwell in inward tranquillity and be calm. Get rid of doubt and perplexity and dwell with a mind filled with faith and conviction." When the disciple is thus enabled to be controlled in mind, he is further instructed in the various techniques of meditation, leading to the higher stages of Samādhi–higher consciousness born of meditative absorption.

Samadhi

Samādhi brings about a synthesis, a total unification and integration, binding together a number of sublime mental states, which not only cleanse completely the mind and keep it one-pointed and steady, like the flame of a lamp in the absence of wind, but cause that inward illumination, called Wisdom, which permits contact with reality, banishing all delusions and folly, ignorance and self-deceptions. With the emergence of this intuitional power, the path leading to spiritual liberation is both illuminated and opened.

Self-transcendence also implies the pursuit of excellence which has been construed again by this great Master-Mind of India, Buddha, as the most purposive venture in life, Pursuit of knowledge has been the pre-occupation of our time. Knowledge, per se, cannot be an exalted virtue though it could be a power, and often a destructive one. Excellence, per contra, is that higher virtue and inward light that brings about transformation and self-mastery and therewith, true happiness and well-being.

Life in the modern society is a strange paradox. While knowledge has increased many-fold, so have the troubles. The evils of modern society seem to have increased in direct proportion to the increase of knowledge. Today humanity's fund of knowledge is fantastic and so is the human bondage.

Unified code

"A tamed mind brings true happiness." said the B··ddha. To tame the mind, it is essential to follow a unified code of morals which entails increasingly the refinement of mind, outlook and behaviour. Pañca Sīla, the Buddha's unified code, consists of a voluntary renunciation of acts of violence and dishonesty, immorality and untruthfulness and the eschewing of all alcoholic and drug addictions. In positive terms, these precepts envisage a life dedicated to humanism, charity, purity, contentment, and rectitude. A life so designed will have no need for any form of escapism expressed through indulgence in sensuality, drugs and drinks. The social implications of such a code is even more significant, since it not only avoids crime but builds a very cultured humanity, for which the need for excellence becomes a vital necessity. Today, humanity, moving as it is, in such great speed, is threatened not only with a loss of direction but is dogged by constant anxiety and uncertainty. A mind which gets disoriented and confused becomes like a boat without a rudder. The culture of mind, as envisaged by the Supremely Enlightened Buddha, constitutes the panacea for ailing humanity.

9
Purification Of Mind*

Bhikkhu Bodhi

An ancient maxim found in the **Dhammapada** sums up the practice of the Buddha's teaching in three simple guidelines to training: to abstain from all evil, to cultivate good, and to purify one's mind. These three principles form a graded sequence of steps progressing from the outward and preparatory to the inward and essential. Each step leads naturally into the one that follows it, and the culmination of the three in purification of mind makes it plain that the heart of Buddhist practice is to be found here.

Purification of mind as understood in the Buddha's teaching is the sustained endeavour to cleanse the mind of defilements, those dark unwholesome mental forces which run beneath the surface stream of consciousness vitiating our thinking, values, attitudes, and actions. The chief among the defilements are the three that the Buddha has termed the "roots of evil" – greed, hatred, and delusion – from which emerge their numerous offshoots and variants: anger and cruelty, avarice and envy, conceit and arrogance, hypocrisy and vanity, the multitude of erroneous views.

Contemporary attitudes do not look favourably upon such notions as defilement and purity, and on first encounter they may strike us as throwbacks to an outdated moralism, valid perhaps in an era when prudery and taboo were dominant, but having no claims upon us emancipated torchbearers of modernity. Admittedly, we

---

* Buddhist Publication Society, Newsletter, No. 4, Summer 1986. 54, Sangharaja Mawatha, Kandy, Sri Lanka.

do not all wallow in the mire of gross materialism and many among us seek our enlightenments and spiritual highs, but we want them on our own terms, and as heirs of the new freedom we believe they are to be won through an unbridled quest for experience without any special need for introspection, personal change, or self-control.

However, in the Buddha's teaching the criterion of genuine enlightenment lies precisely in purity of mind. The purpose of all insight and enlightened understanding is to liberate the mind from the defilements, and Nibbāna itself, the goal of the teaching, is defined quite clearly as freedom from greed, hatred, and delusion. From the perspective of the Dhamma defilement and purity are not mere postulates of a rigid authoritarian moralism but real and solid facts essential to a correct understanding of the human situation in the world.

As facts of lived experience, defilement and purity pose a vital distinction having a crucial significance for those who seek deliverance from suffering. They represent the two points between which the path to liberation unfolds – the former its problematic and starting point, the latter its resolution and end. The defilements, the Buddha declares, lie at the bottom of all human suffering. Burning within as lust and craving, as rage and resentment, they lay to waste hearts, lives, hopes, and civilizations, and drive us blind and thirsty through the round of birth and death. The Buddha describes the defilements as bonds, fetters, hindrances, and knots; thence the path to unbonding, release, and liberation, to untying the knots, is at the same time a discipline aimed at inward cleansing.

The work of purification must be undertaken in the same place where the defilements arise, in the mind itself, and the main method the Dhamma offers for purifying the mind is meditation. Meditation, in the Buddhist training, is neither a quest for self-effusive ecstasies nor a technique of home-applied psychotherapy, but a carefully devised method of mental development – theoretically precise and practically efficient – for attaining inner purity and spiritual freedom. The principal tools of Buddhist meditation are the core wholesome mental factors of energy, mindfulness, concentration, and understanding. But in the systematic practice of meditation, these are strengthened and yoked together in a program of self-purification which aims at extirpating the defilements root and branch so that not even the subtlest unwholesome stirrings remain.

Since all defiled states of consciousness are born from ignorance, the most deeply embedded defilement, the final and ultimate purification of mind is to be accomplished through the instrumentality of wisdom, the knowledge and vision of things as they really are. Wisdom, however, does not arise through chance or random good intentions, but only in a purified mind. Thus in order for wisdom to come forth and accomplish the ultimate purification through the eradication of defilements, we first have to create a space for it by developing a provisional purification of mind – a purification which, though temporary and vulnerable, is still indispensable as a foundation for the emergence of all liberative insight.

The achievement of this preparatory purification of mind begins with the challenge of self-understanding. To eliminate defilements we must first learn to know them, to detect them at work infiltrating and dominating our everyday thoughts and lives. For countless aeons we have acted on the spur of greed, hatred, and delusion, and thus the work of self-purification cannot be executed hastily, in obedience to our demand for quick results. The task requires patience, care, and persistence – and the Buddha's crystal clear instructions. For every defilement the Buddha in his compassion has given us the antidote, the method to emerge from it and vanquish it. By learning these principles and applying them properly, we can gradually wear away the most stubborn inner stains and reach the end of suffering, the "taintless liberation of the mind."

10

SILENCE : Its Ethical Reach And Spiritual Significance*

Dr. R.L. Soni

"If 'speech' is silvern, 'silence' is golden", is an old saying which is too true in many ways. Certainly, silence, as remarked by some one, is about the best antidote to the garrulity of today. There are happily many who practised it in recent times. Some of them reported excellent results in self-control and in ethical and spiritual benefits.

While much damage occurs through indiscretion in speech, no such harm or even regret is possible in the practice of wholesome silence. Vulgarity in speech, disregarding the accepted social conventions of polite behaviour, or the use of imprudent and ill-advised words, is known to alienate relations and to insert a wedge between friends. Also, certainly, tongue can cut more fiercely than a sword. Such a tongue adversely affects chances of success in matters professional and in other activities. On the other hand, silence, besides preventing many an evil, promotes understanding, gives rest to the mind, and peace to the heart. Also, silence makes one know one's strength and weaknesses, and helps to use discretion, thus enabling many a sublime conquest.

Of course, it is not denied that much good can also attend discriminate and restrained talk. Also, speech must not be withheld when capable of doing good. As a matter of fact, it is very essential in worldly pursuits. With speech discreet and purified, one removes

---

* Maha Bodhi Journal, Vol. 72, March-April 1964, pp. 54-58.

misunderstandings and wins affection and regard of one's contacts: one can govern multitudes, and can be markedly sure of success in one's undertakings. But, the fact needs be faced that more often than not the faculty of speech not only errs but also not unoften errs grievously. That explains why the Buddha put emphasis on the 'speech' to be 'right', when He gave to *samma-vaca* (or right speech) an important place – as a matter of fact, priority in the sphere of *sila* (morality) – in His *atthangika-magga* or the Enghtfold Noble Path, which is essential to be trodden to reach the Supreme Goal. For the speech to be right, it has not only to be without malice, lies, rudeness, idle babble, and slander, but also it needs the positively truthful, sweet, straight, and conditioned by loving-kindness. This action of the tongue, whether bad or good, is, however, a *kamma* or action with binding-results, and is termed *Vaci-kamma*. It is with binding results because of the volitions preceding it and the *Vaci-sankhara* or verbal *kamma*-formations following it. Hence, depending on its quality, it is responsible for our promotion or demotion in the scale of phenomenal existences. Thus, our speech has not only ethical significance but also spiritual meaning.

Obviously, wholesome use of speech can elevate us morally and materially: this may mean not only subjective satisfaction but also familial happiness, material benefits, social advantages, and professional gains. This may also help to rise in the scale of the planes of existence, even up to the *Brahma-loka*. On the other hand, faulty use of speech spells handicaps, obstacles, and disadvantages in all these spheres. Whatever, speech is a matter of *kamma* and as such its sphere of influence remains located to the 31 planes of *Samsara*. The only exception to this rule is in case of a Buddha or an *Arahat* (Supreme Saint), who are beyond the sphere of *kamma*-formations, and as such in whom the binding force of *tanha* or craving usually associated with action is utterly absent. They talk out of compassion and without any desire for personal gain or for any craving for results.

In the light of the above observations, if speech is usually a matter of *kammic* 'sowing and reaping', what would be the status of silence in the terminology of *kamma*?

Of course, silence in the sense of verbal silence does not necessarily signify all-round silence. For, while the tongue is silent, the mind might not be: and, even the body might be active, wholesomely or otherwise. Thus, all the same, there will be *kamma* done through the body or the mind–*kāya-kamma* and *mano-kamma*. If silence of the tongue was all in all and enough, all the dumb would be blessed for their mutism. That, however, is not the case: this is so, for, their body is active for *kamma* and their mind perhaps more so and possibly in the wrong direction. It might be argued that is not the silence that is forced by bodily malformation or by 'emptiness of the brain', or by any dysfunction of the faculty of speech that spells virtue, but the silence voluntarily accepted as a means to self-control. Certainly, such a silence is beneficial, morally as well as spiritually, even if practised occasionally at a stretch or daily for a few hours. But, this would be so, specially if it also spelt self-control over the voluntary organs of the body and over the mental trends. In that case, volitions (*cetanā*) which manifest as *kammic* actions of the body, speech, or mind (*kāya, vacī,* and *mano*), shall all be under control.

Certainly, the mind is the most important, it being not only the initiator of all *kamma* but also a potent instrument for navigating the being to the 'Beyond'. The psychic roots of *kamma* are in the mind, these being *lobha, dosa,* and *moha* (greed, hate, and delusion). So long as these are operative, there shall be no safety, even if silence was observed tenaciously and for years. Only when the verbal silence is observed as a means to check the growth and to control the functioning of these unwholesome roots that there arises a situation when these roots begin to decay. Then, in due course, and certainly only after a strenuous process of self-discipline, *lobha* is replaced by *alobha* (greedlessness), *dosa* by *adosa* (hatelessness), and *moha* by *amoha* delusionlessness). When this discipline attains to perfection, the mental activity becomes bereft of *tanhā* (or the force of craving), and as such devoid of *kamma*. That is the state when Truth is completely realised, which spells awakening into the reality of impersonality (*anatta*).

The entire phenomenon is, basically speaking, nothing but a complex of wavelengths, which means 'ebb and flow' or rise and fall in Nature. In a living being, these waves assume a personal meaning and usually take the form of '*Lokadhamma*', expressing as *tanha* (gain) or *alābha* (loss), *yasa* (fame) or *ayasa* (disgrace), *pasaṁsa* (praise) or *ninda* (blame), *sukha* (happiness) or *dukkha* (suffering). However, in the Sage who has awakened to the Truth of *anatta* or impersonality, this personal significance becomes besides the point. Then the silence with the Sage is a matter of waveless silence, so far as are concerned the waves associated with personal biases. Such a Sage prefers silence to speech: as a matter of fact, he is silent through and through in the *kammic* sense, silent bodily, silent in speech, and silent mentally. Hence, he is termed as '*mauni*', meaning 'The Silent One'. When he speaks, he speaks out of compassion for others' wellbeing, without any *kammic* binding whatsoever to himself.

The entire phenomenon, as said above, is basically a matter of waves of energy. As such, it cannot be supremely silent, for, the waves crash and interact, thus producing a variety of sounds, animate as well as inanimate, pleasant as well as otherwise. Even if there be no clash or interaction, they are characterized by certain sounds within or without the range of our acoustic perceptions. Therefore, even if we attain to the highest possible spiritual status in phenomenon, we will, objectively speaking, not be in really waveless silence: this, of course, taking the outer world as a whole. For, the phenomenon will continue with its noise—natural, as of thunder, winds, clashes in matter, flow of fluids, and a variety of animal sounds; as well as artificial, because of the play of music and singing of songs, and because of noisy talks and functions, also because of the working of machines, use of fire-arms, aeroplanes, trains, loud speakers, radios, etc., as well as because of the rabid loqua-city of man and his temper bursting out in politics, quarrels, wars, and in the explosion of bombs and thermonuclear devices. Beyond these sounds, some enchanting, some detestable, and some so so, are the celestial regions, characterised by '*the music of the spheres*'. That too is phenomenal and associated with the 'being', howsoever subtle though. As such, even there utter silence is out of question: at its best, even the soothing and captivating spiritual music is, so to say, deodorant to cover and disguise the unwanted noises. Only when we attain to the realisation of *anatta* or utter 'impersonality', we go beyond all duality, beyond all ideas of personality and of phenomenality. Only the ultra-phenomenal is a matter of *Supreme* and *Real Silence*. That Silence is transdimensional in every sense of the word, and as such is transcendental and concerned with actual *Realisation*. It defies description, which is a matter of tri-dimensional narration and an affair of conditionality or relativity. That SILENCE verily is *Nibbāna*.

11
Vipassanā And Aśoka's Dhamma*

D.C. Ahir

The name and fame of Asoka, the great Emperor of India, is well-known throughout the whole world. Paying tribute to him, H.G. Wells, the great historian of modern times, says:[1] "Amidst the tens of thousands of names of monarchs that crowd the columns of history, their majesties and graciousnesses and serenities and royal highnesses and the like, the name of Asoka shines, and shines almost alone, a star."

Asoka was the grandson of Chandragupta, the founder of the Maurya dynasty. After the death of his father, Bindusara, Asoka ascended the Magadha throne in 273 B.C. His coronation, however, took place in 269 B.C.

Asoka was fortunate in inheriting a well-established empire which included almost the whole of modern India, excepting Orissa and the far South, Pakistan and Afghanistan. To this vast empire, Asoka added Kalinga (modern Orissa), which he conquered after a bloody war. The large-scale massacre in the Kalinga war deeply influenced his mind and brought revolution in his character. With this event, his outlook, both in his personal and public life, changed. Consequently, he was drawn to the mild teachings of the Compassionate Buddha. After adopting the Buddha's teachings, he declared that henceforth he would prefer 'Dhamma-Vijaya' to 'Rājya-Vijaya'. In other words, he took a vow to win the hearts

* The Seminar on Vipassana Meditation, Vipassana Research Institute, Igatpuri, Maharashtra, India, December 1986.

of the people, both inside and outside the borders of his empire, by persuasion and love, instead of by the use of force and sword.

Asoka speaks to us through his inscriptions on the rocks and pillars which have since been discovered at 40 places in India (34), Nepal (2), Pakistan (2) and Afghanistan (2). All the inscriptions found in India and Nepal are composed in various forms of Prākrit and are written in the Brāhmī script. The two inscriptions at Shahbazgarhi and Mansehra in Pakistan are written in Kharoshthī. An inscription discovered at Kandhar in Afghanistan is bi-lingual, in Greek and Aramaic. In all the records, Asoka refers to himself as *'Devānāmpiya Piyadasi Rājā'* (the Beloved of the Gods, the king Piyadasi). Only in two versions of Minor[2] Rock Edict I, the king's name is mentioned.

In his edicts, Asoka time and again refers to *'Dhamma'* and exhorts one and all to inculcate the practice of Dhamma. What was meant by 'Dhamma' by Asoka has been a subject of comment by the historians. Some scholars have even opined that 'Asoka's Dhamma' was his own innovation and it had nothing to do with the 'Buddha-Dhamma'. This is not a correct interpretation. Asoka propagated Dhamma as taught by the Buddha. This is very well confirmed by the evidence that Asoka himself provides in his edicts.

In one of the earliest rock edicts to be issued by Asoka, he says:[3]

"A little more than two years and a half passed since I am avowedly a lay follower of the Buddha. But I was not vigorously exerting myself in the cause of Dhamma for the first one year. However, it is little more than a year that I am devotedly attached to the Sangha and exerting myself vigorously".

The above edict, now known as Minor Rock Edict I has been discovered at as many as 14 places in India. This means that Asoka gave widest publicity to his increasing devotion to the Buddha's teachings.

In the third Minor Rock Edict, which has been discovered only at Bairat near Jaipur, Rajasthan, Asoka says:"[4]

"King Piyadasi of Magadha salutes the monks of the
Sangha, wishes them good health and comfort in their
movement, and addresses them in the following words.
It is known to you, Venerable Sirs, how far extends my
reverence for and faith in the Buddha, the Dhamma
and the Sangha. Whatever, Venerable Sirs, has been
said by the Lord Buddha, all that is well-said. But
Venerable Sirs, I deem it proper to speak out what
appears to me the way as to how the true Dhamma
may be of long duration."

Asoka then goes on to list seven texts[5] of Dhamma (for details
please see note 5), and directs that the monks and nuns may
constantly listen to and remember these texts. Likewise lay men
and lay women too.

Asoka not only suggested constant study of certain texts by
the monks, nuns and the laity, he also took keen interest in the
affairs of the Sangha. He even endeavoured to check schism in
the Sangha. In the Minor Pillar Edict I found at Allahabad-Kosam,
Sanchi and Sarnath, Asoka addresses the monks and nuns in these
words:[6]

"No one is to cause dissension in the Order. Whoever
creates a schism in the Order, whether monk or nun,
is to be dressed in white garments, and to be put in a
place not inhabited by monks or nuns. For it is my wish
that the Order should remain united and endure for
long."

Asoka's own words, quoted above, make it clear that he was
a devout follower of the Buddha. Not only he refers to the Buddha,
the Dhamma and the Sangha, the Buddha is also represented in
the Edicts by the well-known symbol of the White Elephant[7] which
is indicated by an inscription at Girnar at the end of R.E. XIII, and
represented by a figure cut on the rock at Dhauli, and incised at
Kalsi with the label *'gajatame'*, "the most perfect elephant." The
elephant stands for the Buddha's descent on earth as His mother
saw in dream, before conception, a white elephant entering her
womb. The four animals topping the Asokan pillars are: the Elephant,

the Bull, the Horse and the Lion. These animals were chosen by Asoka as they are associated with the Buddha. The Elephant typifies Conception, the Bull indicates Nativity, Buddha's birth as a human being, the Horse stands for the Buddha's Renunciation, and the Lion represents Buddha as the great Teacher. Four Lions facing four directions indicate that the Buddha (Sākya-simha) preached in all the directions and to all the mankind.

Asoka's devotion to the Buddha is evident from some other facts also, such as, his pilgrimage to the holy shrines; his observance of uposatha;* and convening the Third Council at Pataliputra. In spite of all this, however, Asoka nowhere in his edicts calls it 'Buddha-Dhamma'. He merely calls it 'Dhamma' or 'Dharma' everywhere. The essence of Dhamma has been elucidated by Asoka in five principal edicts, viz., three rock edicts and two pillar edicts.

In the third Major Rock Edict found at Girnar in Gujarat, Asoka defines Dhamma in these words:

"It is good to be obedient to one's mother and father, friends and relatives, to be generous to brāhmaṇas and śramaṇas, it is good not to kill living beings, it is good not only to spend little, but to own the minimum of property."

In the fourth Major Rock Edict, at Girnar again, Asoka says:[9]

"Through his (Asoka's) instruction in Dhamma, abstention from killing and non-injury to living beings, defeerence to relatives, brāhmaṇas and śramaṇas, obedience to mother and father, and obedience to elders have all increased as never before for centuries."

Again in the Major Rock Edict No. XI found at Kalsi, near Paonta in Himachal Pradesh, Asoka says:[10]

"There is no gift comparable to the gift of Dhamma, the praise of Dhamma, the sharing of Dhamma, fellowship in Dhamma. And this is—good behaviour towards slaves and servants, obedience to mother and

---

* Certain days for the observance of eight precepts etc.

father, generosity towards friends, acquaintances, and
relatives and towards *śramaṇas* and *brāhmaṇas*, and
abstention from killing living beings."
Of the seven Major Pillar Edicts, Dhamma is specifically
defined in two edicts. In edict No. II, on the Topra Pillar now
standing at Ferozshah Kotla, Delhi, Asoka says:[11]

> "The practices of Dhamma are meritorious. But what
> does Dhamma consist of? It consists of the least amount
> of sin, many virtuous deeds, compassion, liberality,
> truthfulness and purity."

Again in edict No. VII on the same Delhi-Topra Pillar, Asoka
says:[12]

> "My intention is that the noble deeds of Dhamma and
> the practice of Dhamma, which consist of compassion,
> liberality, truthfulness, purity, gentleness and goodness,
> will thus be promoted among men."

The Asokan Edicts were primarily addressed to the people
in general, the lay men and lay women. Hence, without referring
to the purely Buddhistic terms like the Four Noble Truths, the Noble
Eightfold Path and *Nirvaṇa*, Asoka lists in simple language the
virtues, the path that a lay person ought to follow. And while doing
so, he lists the virtues keeping in view the 'layman's code of
conduct' as laid down by the Buddha in the Sigāla - Sutta[13] (No.
31 of the Dīgha-Nikāya). Asoka preaches the ethical discipline,
the virtues which lead to the attainment of happiness in this world
and the next. He preached these virtues to all classes of people,
both rich and poor, and endeavoured to inculcate the spirit of true
Dhamma - self-control, purity of thought, compassion, truthfulness
and goodness to all. Moral foundation for a nation is a must for
material, mental and spiritual rise. And this is what Asoka
endeavoured to achieve through Dhamma.

There are two forms of meditation. One form is *Samatha,*
Calm or development of mental concentration. The other form is
Vipassanā, Insight, which was discovered by Buddha at the time
of His Enlightenment. *Vipassanā* means to see things as they really
are. It aims at "exposing the truth of impermanency, the suffering,

and the unsubstantial nature of all material and mental phenomena of existence."[14] (*anicca, dukkha, anatta*). Vipassanā ultimately leads to the complete liberation of mind, to the realization of the Ultimate Truth, Nirvāṇa.

Asoka nowhere refers to Vipassanā, yet it is felt that besides constant emphasis on the virtuous living (*sīla*), he must have arranged to preach and teach the people the deeper aspects of the Dhamma. In the Pillar Edict VII[15] Asoka speaks of 'manifold Dhamma instructions' and orders his officers to explain the same in detail to the people. His manifold Dhamma instructions must have included instructions on practising the Dhamma based on *Sīla* (Morality), *Samādhi* (Meditation - mastery over mind), and *Paññā* (Wisdom); the three essential ingredients of the Vipassanā meditation. Some indication of this is available in the selection of the seven Texts recommended by Asoka for study by the monks, nuns and the lay people. If we just have a look at the three *suttas* chosen by Asoka from the Sutta-Nipāta, it is apparent that all the three *Suttas* recommended by Asoka lay emphasis on *meditation.*[16]

Even if it is disputed that Asoka's Dhamma instructions did not cover the Vipassanā technique as such, yet it cannot be denied that the Dhamma preached by him was the universal Dhamma and was fully in accord with the spirit of Vipassanā. Asoka's Dhamma consisted of the virtues of: Kindness (*dayā*), liberality (*dānam*), truthfulness (*satyam*), inner and outer purity (*śaucam*), gentleness (*mārdavam*), saintliness (*sādhutā*), self-control (*smayama*), purity of heart (*bhāvaúddhi*), gratitude (*kritajnatā*), firm devotion (*driḍhabhakti*), and attachment to morality (*dhamma-rati*). Thus it was the Dhamma or *Sila, samādhi* and *paññā,* that leads one from darkness to light, from passion to dispassion, from turmoil to tranquillity.

Buddha's teachings stand on three pillars – the Buddha, the Dhamma and the Sangha. Of these, Dhamma has naturally the central position because it is only the practice of Dhamma which enables a person to attain *Nirvāṇa*, the highest goal. The late Sayagyi U Ba Khin, the great Vipassanā Teacher of modern Burma (the country that preserved the Vipassanā technique in its pristine purity), says,[17] "There are three gems, the Buddha, the Dhamma, and the Sangha. Of these three gems, the most important is the Dhamma because without the Dhamma, a Buddha cannot arise."... "Buddha is what is called the aggregate of the *Dhammakāya*, the embodiment of the Dhamma." Likewise, Asoka too speaks of his respect for and faith in the Buddha, the Dhamma and the Sangha, but the all-pervasive force in his inscriptions is 'Dhamma'. Significantly enough, Asoka uses the term *'Dhamma'* as many as 125 times[18] in his inscriptions. For him, the practice of Dhamma was the most vital thing. So he "governed the people according to Dhamma, administered justice according to Dhamma, caused happiness to them according to Dhamma, and protected them according to Dhamma[19]." Thus the sound of the dhamma drum (*dhamma-ghosa*) reverberated throughout his empire. In brief, ... Asoka's *Dhamma-Vijaya* consisted "in the expression of goodwill and assurance of territorial integrity, the friendly acts of public utility, and advancement of the cause of humanity through piety."

A Vipassanā student cultivates the four Sublime States (*Brahma - Vihāra*) of *Mettā* - Loving-kindness; *Karuṇā* - Compassion; *Muditā* - Sympathetic Joy; and *Upekkhā* - Equanimity or Evenmindedness. In tune with the *Metta-bhāvanā* or *Maṅgala-maitri* of the Vipassanā tradition, Asoka says,[20] "There is no greater duty for me than doing good to the whole world." (Major Rock Edict VI). The benevolent Asoka goes on to say:[21] "All men are my children. I wish happiness and welfare to all men, as I would wish to my own children." (First Separate Rock Edict - Dhauli Text). For the material welfare of his subjects, Asoka undertook the provision of public works of utility on an unprecedented scale. And influenced by the virtues of *Mettā* and *Karuṇā*, Asoka ordered abolition of sacrifical slaughter of animals; *samajas* (merry-making of a kind, accompanied by animal fights and feasting with consumption of meat etc); meat diet for the royal household; "tours of pleasure" accompanied by hunting and other similar amusements.

While keen to preach and propagate the marvellous teachings of the Buddha, Asoka showed equal respect for the various religious sects. Even though an ardent follower of the Buddha himself, he asks no one to adopt Buddhism. Similar is the approach of the modern Vipassanā teachers. Goenkaji says,[22] "When an Enlightened One teaches Dhamma, it is always pure Dhamma, free from sectarianism. Pure Dhamma is universal truth. Pure Dhamma is good for all, beneficial to all. It is not necessary that one should call oneself a Buddhist in order to experience the benefits of the Dhamma taught by the Buddha . . . . What really matters is one's actual practice of Dhamma."

A Vipassanā student is reminded time and again during the Dhamma discourses that in order to practise true Dhamma, he should shun ritualism and avoid useless religious ceremonies. According to Asoka also, "the auspicious ceremonies performed on the occasions of illness, the weddings, the birth etc. are trivial and meaningless."[23] By the third century B.C. the relic-worship or the *caitya* - worship had come into vogue amongst the followers of the Buddha. Asoka himself is said to have built as many as 84,000 *stūpas* throughout his empire, and some of these *stūpas* had even the sacred relics of the Buddha enshrined in them, yet, significantly enough, he does not refer to the relic-worship or the like in his inscriptions. For, in his view,[24] "The quintessence of Dhamma consisted in *sīla* or good conduct, and not in creed, rituals, ceremonies or worship."

In sum, the records of Asoka were not to commemorate his military triumph over Kalinga and other secular achievements but they were intended to "convey the lofty message of an enlightened seer for eternal good and happiness." Asoka wanted the Dhamma to illumine the path of all to the Ultimate Goal, *Nirvāṇa*, reaching which one leaves behind all that is *dukkha*; all that is born of *lobha* (greed), *dosa* (hatred), and *moha* (delusion) and all that is rooted in *avijjā* or Ignorance.

Asoka, also called *Dhammāsoka* or *Dharmarāja*, "the King of Dharma" passed away in 232 B.C. but the respect for Dhamma propagated by him endured for a long time. For centuries, "the followers of the Buddha's teachings have called their faith simply *Dharma*[25] or at the most '*Saddharma*' or '*Sadharma*' and to have styled themselves as '*Dharmin*' or 'Sadharmin'."

Notes

1. H.G. Wells, The Outline of History, p 402.

2. Minor Rock Edict I, Maski (Andhra Pradesh) and Gujarra (Madhya Pradesh) texts. cf. D.C. Sircar, Inscriptions of Asoka, Delhi, 1957, pp. 34-35.

3. D.C. Sircar, Inscriptions of Asoka, Delhi, 1957, Minor Rock Edict I, p 33. This edict has been found at Sahasaram (Bihar), Ahroura (U.P.), Bairat (Rajasthan), Bahapur (Delhi), Rupnath, Gujarra (Madhya Pradesh), Brahmagiri, Jatinga-Ramesvara, Siddhapura (Karnataka) and Maski, Yerragudi, Gavimath, Palkigundu, Rajula-Mandagiri (Andhra Pradesh).

4. Sircar, Inscriptions of Asoka, Minor Rock Edict III, p. 38.

5. Sircar translates the seven texts listed by Asoka as under: the Exaltation of Discipline; the Noble States of Living; the Fears to Come; the Song of the Hermit; the Discourse on the State of a Hermit; the Questions of Upatishya; and the Exhortation to Rahula, which was delivered by the Lord Buddha on the subject of falsehood. Sujitkumar Mukho-padhyaya identifies these texts with the following texts in the Tipitaka:

   Vinaya-samukase - Vinaya-samukkansa - "select passages from Vinaya", of Atthavasa-vagga in the Anguttara-Nikaya, 1.98-100.

   Aliya-vasanj - Ariya-vasa (dasa) "The excellent state of mind", Digha-Nikaya, III, 269, 291; Anguttara-Nikaya, V. 29.

   Anagata-bhayani (panca), Anguttara, III. 100-110. Muni-gatha - Muni-sutta, Sutta-Nipata, 1.12. (sutta), Moneya-sute - Nalaka-sutta, ibid., III II (sutta). Upatisa-pasine - Sariputta-sutta, "What Upatissa (Sariputta) asked", ibid., IV. 16.

   Laghulovade - Rahulovada, "Instruction to Rahula", of. Ambalatthika-Rahulovada-sutta, Majjhima Nikaya, 1. 414-20. of. Sujitkumar Mukhipadhyaya. The Asokavadana, Sahitya Akademi, New Delhi, 1963, Appendix B. Asoka Inscriptions, p. 154.

6. Romila Thapar, Asoka and the Decline of the Mauryas, Delhi, 1973, Appendix V, A Translation of the Edicts of Asoka, p 262.

7. R.K. Mookerji, Asoka, Delhi, 3rd edition, 1962, pp. 61-62.

8. Romila Thapar, Asoka and the Decline of the Mauryas 3rd Major Rock Edict, p. 251.

9. Ibid., 4th Major Rock Edict, p. 251.

10. Ibid., 6th Major Rock Edict, pp 254-255.

11. Sircar, Inscriptions of Asoka, Pillar Edict II, p. 68.

12. Ibid., Pillar Edict VII, pp. 75-76.

13. The six sets of reciprocal duties enumerated in the Sigala-sutta, No. 31 of Digha-nikaya, are: between parents and children; between pupils and teachers; between husband and wife; friends and companions; masters and servants; and lastly the laity and the Sangha. In each case, there are five duties, except in the case of Sangha's duties to householders, which are six.

14. Nyanatiloka, Buddhist Dictionary - Manual of Buddhist Terms and Discourses, Fourth edition, Buddhist Publication Society, Kandy, Srilanka, 1980, p. 245.

15. Sujitkumar Mukhopadhyaya, The Asokavadana, Appendix B, Asoka Inscriptions, Pillar Edict VII, p. 147.

16. The following three verses are taken from "The Sacred Books of the East - Edited by F. Max Muller, Volume X, Part II - the Sutta-Nipata - Translated from Pali by V. Fausboll, Motilal Banarsidass, Delhi, 1973 edition:

"6. The man who has the strength of understanding is endowed with virtue and (holy) works, is composed, delights in meditation, is thoughtful, free from ties, free from harshness, and free from passion, him the wise style a Muni". (211)

– 1.12 - Muni Sutta, p. 34.

"31. Applying himself to meditation, and being wise, let him find his pleasure in the outskirts of the wood, let him meditate at the root of a tree enjoying himself." (709).

– III. 11-Nalaka Sutta, p. 129.

"18. Let him be with downcast eyes, and not prying, devoted to meditation, very watchful; having acquired equanimity let him with a composed mind cut off the seat of doubt, and misbehaviour." (972).

– IV. 16-Sariputta Sutta, p. 182.

17. Vipassana Journal, Special Number, 19th January 1983, Hyderabad, Sayings of Sayagyi, last page.

18. The term 'Dhamma' is used by Asoka 57 times in the 14 Major Rock Edicts, and 48 times in the 7 Major Pillar Edicts, and 20 times in other inscriptions.

19. D.C. Sircar, Inscriptions of Asoka, Pillar Edict I, p. 67

20. B.M. Barua, Asoka and His Inscriptions, Calcutta, 1968, 3rd edition, Major Rock Edict VI (p. 246).

21. Sircar, Inscriptions of Asoka, Rock Edict XV and XVI, pp. 56 and 59.

22. Vipassana Journal, Special Number, January 1983, opposite page 67.

23. Sircar, Inscriptions of Asoka, Rock Edict IX, p. 47.

24. Amulyachandra Sen, Asoka's Edicts, Calcutta, 1956, p. 34.

25. N.N. Vasu, Modern Budhism and its followers in Orissa, 1911, pp 150-151. Some Buddhists of Orissa (Kalinga) still call themselves as 'Mahima-Dharmis' or followers of the Praiseworthy Dharma.

12

Place Of Jhāna And Samādhi In Theravāda Buddhism*

Ven. Henepola Gunaratana

In the discourses the Buddha says that just as in the great occean there is but one taste, the taste of salt, so in his doctrine and discipline there is but one taste, the taste of freedom (*vinuttirasa*). The taste of freedom that flavors the Buddha's doctrine and discipline is the taste of spiritual freedom, and it is to the full experience of this taste that the entire teaching of Buddha is directed. Spiritual freedom, from the Buddhist perspective, means freedom from suffering. The problem of suffering is the well-spring out of which the whole current of Buddhist teaching arises : freedom from suffering is the end towards which it moves. Thus the Buddha could say throughout his minstry : "Previously, monks, as also now I make known only suffering and the cessation of suffering."

This focal concern with the issue of suffering is evident from the formula of the four Noble Truths in which the Buddha summed up his doctrine. The formula of the Four Noble Truths deals entirely with the problem of suffering, looked at from four different angles. The first truth exposes the forms and the range of suffering. It shows suffering to be an inextricable ingredient of life itself, tied on the physical side to the vital processes of birth, aging, sickness and death, cropping up on the psychological side as sorrow, grief,

---

* Maha Bodhi journal, April-June 1981, pp. 87-96 Ven. H. Ganaratana is the author of "The Path of Serenity and Insight : An Explanation of the Buddhist Jhanas. Delhi, 1985.

dejection, and despair. Even more, in the Buddha's picture of the world the mass of suffering becomes multiplied to infinite proportions due to the fact of rebirth. The cycle of pain and sorrow does not turn only once; for all but the enlightened it turns over and over through beginningless time in the form of *saṁsara,* the round of repeated becoming.

Having exposed the range and modes of suffering in the first Noble Truth, in the remaining three the Buddha points out the cause of suffering, its cessation, and the way to its cessation. The cause is craving, the insatiable drive for enjoyment and existence that keeps the wheel of rebirths in constant motion. The cessation of suffering is the reversal of this genetic relation, the complete abandoning and destruction of craving. The way to the end of suffering is the middle way of ethical and mental training that avoids all extremes of conduct and views–the Noble Eightfold Path made up of right view, right intention, right speech, right action, right livelihood, right effort, right mindfulness, and right concentration.

Whereas the first three truths provide the doctrinal perspective of the Buddha's teaching, the fourth truth, the truth of the path, prescribes its practical regimen. This regimen focusses upon personal experience. The Buddha does not come into our midst as a savior descended from on high. He comes as an enlightened teacher, a man who has found the way to the end of suffering and who points the way out to others. The path itself every man must follow for himself. It is each man's own delusions and defilements that chain him to the cycle of suffering, and again each man's own efforts at inner purification that pave the road to his deliverance. Since bondage ultimately springs from ignorance (*avijjā*) the key to liberation, the Buddha declares, is found in wisdom (*pannā*), a wisdom which must be generated inwardly as an immediate personal understanding of the basic truths of existence. The Dhamma is *paccattaṁ veditabbo vinnūhi* "to be realized by the wise within themselves."

It is because personal realization of truth is needed to reach the end of suffering that meditation assumes a position of such crucial importance in the Buddhist formulation of the liberating path.

Meditation, for Buddhism, is the means of generating the inner understanding required for deliverance from suffering. Its diversity of techniques stems from the differences in the people to be taught, but its purpose and procedure is the same for all: to produce that purity of mind and clarity of vision needed for the liberating wisdom to arise.

The methods of meditation taught in the Pali Buddhist tradition are based on the Buddha's own experience, forged by him in the course of his own quest for enlightenment. They are designed to re-create in the disciple who practises them the same essential discovery the Buddha himself made when he sat beneath the Bodhi tree, the discovery of the Four Noble Truths.

The various subjects and methods of meditation expounded in the Pali scriptures divide into two inter-related systems. One is called the development of serenity (samathabhāvanā) the other the development of insight (vipassanābhāvanā). The former also goes under the name of the development of concentration (samādhibhāvanā), the latter under the name of the development of wisdom (paññābhavanā). The practice of serenity-meditation aims at developing a calm, concentrated, unified state of consciousness as a means of experiencing inner peace and generating wisdom. The practice of insight-meditation aims at gaining direct understanding of the real nature of phenomena. Of the two, the development of insight is regarded by Buddhism as the essential key to liberation, the direct antidote to the ignorance underlying bondage and suffering. Whereas serenity-meditation is recognized as common to both Buddhist and non-Buddhist contemplative disciplines, insight-meditation is held to be the unique discovery of the Buddha and an unparallelled feature of his path. However, because the growth of insight presupposes a certain degree of concentration (samādhi), and serenity-meditation serves to secure this concentration, the development of serenity claims an incontestable place in the Buddhist meditative process. Together the two types of meditation work to make the mind a fit instrument for enlightenment. With his mind unified by means of the development of serenity, made sharp and bright by the development of insight, the meditator can proceed unobstructed to reach the end of suffering.

Focal to both systems of meditation, though belonging inherently to the side of serenity, is a set of meditative attainments called the four *jhānas*. The Pali word *jhāna* has been rendered by translators into English in various ways–as "meditation," which to us seems too general; "rapture" and "ecstasy," which suggest a degree of elation and exuberance inappropriate to the higher *jhānas*; as "musing," which is too weak and archaic; and as "trance," which misleadingly implies a subnormal state, quite the opposite of *jhāna*. The word "absorption," used by some translators, is the most suitable of the lot, but that is needed for the Pali *appanā*, which includes the *jhānas* and corresponds closely to "absorption" in literal meaning. For obvious reasons, therefore, we prefer to leave the Pali *jhāna* untranslated.

The *jhānas* themselves are states of deep mental unification characterized by a total immersion of the mind in its object. They result from the centering of the mind upon a single object with such a degree of attention that the discursive activity of thought is slowed down and eventually stopped. The members of the fourfold set of *jhānas* are named simply after their numerical position in the series : the first *jhāna*, the second *jhāna*, the third *jhāna*, and the fourth *jhāna*. The four appear repreatedly in the suttas described by a stock formula showing their process of attainment;

Herein, monks, a monk, quite secluded from sense pleasures, secluded from un-wholesome states of mind, enters and dwells in the first *jhāna*, which is accompanied by applied thought and sustained thought with rapture and happiness born of seclusion.

With the subsiding of applied thought and sustained thought he enters and dwells in the second *jhāna*, which has internal confidence and unification of mind, is without applied thought and sustained thought, and is filled with rapture and happiness born of concentration.

With the fading away of rapture, he dwells in equanimity, mindful and discerning; and he experiences in his own person that happiness of which the noble ones say I 'Happily lives he who is equanimous and mindful'–thus he enters and dwells in the third *jhāna*.

With the abandoning of pleasure and pain, and with the previous disappearance of joy and grief, he enters and dwells in the fourth *jhāna* which has neither-pain-nor-pleasure and has purity of mindfulness due to equanimity.[1]

To attain the *jhānas,* as the passage shows, the meditator must begin by eliminating the unwholesome mental states obstructing inner collectedness. These are generally grouped together as the five hindrances (*pañcanīvaranā*) sensual desire, ill will, sloth and torpor, restlessness and worry, and doubt. The mind's absorption on its object is brought about by five opposing mental states–applied thought, sustained thought, rapture, happiness and one-pointedness called the *jhāna* factors (*jhānaṅgāni*) because they lift the mind to the level of the first *jhāna* and remain there as its defining components.

After reaching the first *jhāna* the ardent meditator can go on to reach the higher *jhānas.* This is done by eliminating the coarser factors in each *jhāna,* those that remain being in each case the defining factors of the successive *jhānas*. In this way the meditator can move from the first *jhāna* up to the fourth. Beyond the four jhānas lies another fourfold set of higher meditative states which deepen the element of serenity developed in the *jhanas.* These attainments, known as the immaterial states (*āruppā*) because they correspond ontologically to the immaterial realms of existence, are the base of boundless space, the base of boundless consciousness, the base of nothingness, and the base of neither perception nor non-perception. In the Pali commentaries this set comes to be called the four immaterial *jhānas* (*arūpajhāna*), the four preceding stages being renamed, for the sake of clarity, the four fine material *jhānas* (*rūpajjhāna*). Often the two sets are joined together under the collective title of the eight *jhānas* or the eight attainments (*aṭṭhasamapattiya*).

The four *jhānas* and four *aruppās* appear initially as mundane states of deep serenity pertaining to the preliminary stage of the

Buddhist path. On this level they help provide the base of concentration needed for wisdom to arise. But the four *jhānas* again re-appear in a later stage as the development of the path, arising in direct association with wisdom. They are then designated the supramundane (*lokuttara*) *jhānas*. These supramundane *jhānas* are the levels of concentration pertaining to the four degrees of enlightenment-experience called the supramundane paths (*lokuttara-magga*) and the stages of deliverance resulting from them, the four fruits (*phala*). Finally, even after full liberation is achieved, the mundane *jhānas* can still remain as attainments available to the liberated person, part of his untrammeled contemplative experience.

The Importance of Jhānas

The importance of the *jhānas* in the Buddhist path to deliverance can readily be gauged from the frequency with which they are mentioned throughout the suttas. The *jhānas* figure prominently both in the Buddha's own experience and in his exhortation to disciples. In his childhood, while attending an annual ploughing festival, the future Buddha spontaneously entered the first *jhāna*. It was the memory of this childhood incident, many years later after his futile pursuit of austerities, that revealed to him the way to enlightenment during his period of despondency.[2] After taking his seat on the banks of the Nerañjarā the Buddha entered the four *jhānas* immediately before directing his mind to the threefold knowledge that issued in his enlightenment.[3] Throughout his active career the four *jhānas* remained "his heavenly dwelling" (*dibbavihāra*) to which he resorted in order to live happily and here now.[4] His understanding of the corruption, purification and emergence in the *jhānas* and other meditative attainments is one of his ten powers which enabled him to turn the matchless wheel of the Dhamma.[5] Just before his passing away the Buddha entered the eight attainments in direct and reverse order; the passing away itself took place directly from the fourth *jhāna*.[6]

The Buddha is constantly seen in the *suttas* encouraging his disciples to develop *jhāna*. The four *jhānas* are invariably included in the complete course of training laid down for disciples.[7] They figure in the training as the discipline of higher consciousness (*adhicittasikkhā*), right concentration (*sammā samādhi*) of the Noble Eightfold Path, and the faculty and power of concentration (*samādhindriya, smādhibala*). Though a vehicle of dry insight can be found, indications are that this path is not an easy one, lacking the aid of the powerful serenity available to the practitioner of *jhāna*. The way of the *jhāna* attainer seems by comparison smoother and more pleasurable.[8]

The Buddha points to the bliss of the *jhānas* as his alternative to sense pleasures. He says:

There are, Cunda, four pursuits of pleasure which lead to ultimate disenchantment, dispassion, cessation, peace, direct knowledge, enlightenment, and *nibbāna*. Which four? Here, Cunda, secluded from sense pleasures, a monk enters and dwells in the first *jhāna*...the second *jhāna*...the third *jhāna*...the fourth *jhāna*.[9]

His own disciples live devoted to these four pursuits of pleasure, and for them four fruits and benefits are to be expected, namely, attainment of the four stages of deliverance–stream-entry, once-returning, non-returning, and arahatship.[10] Just as the river Ganges slopes, inclines, and flows to the east, a bhikkhu who develops and cultivates the four *jhānas* slopes, flows, and inclines to *nibbāna*.[11] The Buddha even refers to the four *jhānas* figuratively (*pariyāyena*) as a kind of nibbāna; he calls them immediately visible *nibbāna*, final *nibbāna*, a factor of *nibbāna*, and *nibbāna* here and now.

Etymology of Jhāna

The great Buddhist commentator Bhadantātariya Buddhaghosa traces the Pali word *Jhāna* (Skt. *dhyāna*) to two verbal forms. One, the etymologically correct derivation, is the verb *jhāyati*, meaning to think or to meditate. Buddhaghosa explains: "By means of this yogins meditate, thus it is called *jhāna* ... The meaning is that they cognize a given object."[12] The commentator offers in addition a more playful derivation of *jhāna*, intended to illuminate its function rather than its verbal source. This derivation traces the word *jhāna* to the verb *jhāpeti* meaning to burn up", the reason being: "It burns up opposing states, thus it is called *jhāna*."[13] The purport of this second account is that *jhāna* "burns up" or destroys the mental defilements preventing the development of serenity and insight.

Buddhoghosa says that *jhāna* has the characteristic mark of contemplation (*upanijjhāna*). Contemplation, he states, is twofold; the contemptation of the object (*ārmmanūpani-jhāna*) and the contemplation of the characteristics of phenomena (*lakkhanūpanijjhāna*). The former type of contemplation is exercised by the eight attainments of serenity together with their access, since these contemplate the object taken as the basis for developing concentration. For this reason these attainments, particularly the first four, are given the name "*jhāna*" in the mainstream of Pali meditative exposition. However, Buddhaghosa also allows that the term "*jhāna*" can be extended loosely to insight (*vipassanā*), the path (*magga*), and fruits (*phala*), on the ground that these perform the work of contemplating the characteristics:

> Here, insight contemplates the characteristics of impermanence, [suffering and selflessness.] Insight's task of contemplation is perfected by the path, thus the path is called the contemplation of characteristics. The fruit contemplates the actual characteristic of cessation, thus it is called the contemplation of characteristics.[14]

In brief the twofold meaning of *jhāna* as "contemplation" and "burning up" can be brought into connection with the meditative process as follows. By fixing his mind on the object the meditator reduces and eliminates the lower mental qualities such as the five hindrances and promotes the growth of the higher qualities such as the *jhāna* factors. These, as they emerge, fix upon the object with increasing force, leading the mind to complete absorption in the object. Then, by contemplating the characteristics of phenomena with insight, the meditator eventually reaches the suparmundane *jhāna* of the four paths. With this *jhāna* he burns up the defilements and attains the liberating experience of the fruits.

Jhāna and Samādhi

In the vocabulary of Buddhist meditation the word *jhāna* is closely connected with another word, *samādhi*, generally rendered by "concentration." *Samādhi* derives from the prefixed verbal root *samā-dhā*, meaning to collect or to bring together, thus suggesting the concentration or unification of the mind. The word *samādhi* is almost interchangeable with the word *samatha*, "serenity", though the latter comes from a different root, *sam* (Skt. *śam)*, meaning "to become calm."

In the suttas *samādhi* is defined as mental one-pointedness, *cittass'ekaggatā*,[15] and this definition is followed through with technically psycholoical rigor in the Abhidhamma. The Abhidhamma treats one-pointedness as a distinct mental factor (*cetasika*) present in every state of consciousness. It is a universal mental concomitant with the function of unifying the mind upon its object, ensuring that each state of consciousness takes one and only one object. Those occasions of one-pointedness which go beyond the bare stabilizing of the mind on an object to give the mind some degree of steadiness and non-distraction are subsumed under the name *samādhi*. Thus the Dhammasaṅgani equates these more prominent types of one-pointedness with a string of synonyms inclusive of serenity (*samatha*), the faculty of concentration (*samādhindriya*), and the power of concentration (*samādhibala*). From this strict psychological standpoint (*samādhi*) can be present in unwholesome states of consciousness as well as in wholesome and neutral states. In its unwholesome forms it is called "wrong concentration" (*micchāsamādhi*), in its wholesome forms "right concentration" (*sammāsamādhi*).

As a technical term in expositions on the practice of meditation, however, *samādhi* is limited to one-pointedness of the wholesome kind. Bhadantācariya Buddhaghosa, in the *Visuddhimagga*, defines *samādhi* as wholesome one-pointedness of mind (*kusalacittass' ekaggatā*), and even here we can understand from the context that it is only the wholesome one-pointedness involved in the deliberate transmutation of the mind to a heightened level of calm that is intended by the word *samādhi*.[16] Buddhaghosa explains *samādhi* etymologically as "the centering of consciousness and consciousness concomitants evenly and rightly on a single object."[17] He calls it "the state is virtue of which consciousness and its concomitants remain evenly and rightly on a single object, undistracted and unscattered."[18]

Despite the preciseness of this definition, the word *samādhi* is used in the Pali literature on meditation with varying degrees of specificity of meaning. In the narrowest sense, as defined by Buddhaghosa, it denotes the particular mental factor responsible for the concentrating of the mind, namely, one-pointedness. In a wider sense it can signify the states of unified consciousness that result from the strengthening of concentration, i.e. the meditative attainments of serenity and the stages leading up to them. And in a still wider sense the word *samādhi* can be applied to the method of practice used to produce and cultivate those refined states of concentration, here being equivalent to the development of serenity (*samathabhāvanā*).

It is in the second sense that *samādhi* and *jhāna* come closest in meaning, sharing to a large extent the same reference. The Buddha equates right concentration with the four *jhānas,* and in doing so allows concentration to encompass the meditative attainments signified by the *jhānas.* However, even though *jhāna* and *samādhi* can overlap in denotation, certain differences in their suggested and contextual meanings prevent unqualified identification of the two terms. Firstly, behind the Buddha's use of the *jhāna* formula to explain right concentration lies a more technical understanding of the terms. According to this understanding *samādhi* can be narrowed down in range to signify only one factor, the most prominent in the *jhāna,* namely one-pointedness, while the *jhāna* itself must be seen as encompassing the state of consciousness in its entirety, or at least the whole group of mental factors individuating that meditative state as a *jhāna.*

In the second place, when *samādhi* is considered in its broader meaning it involves a wider range of reference than *jhāna.* The Pali exegetical tradition recognizes three levels of *samādhi*.[19] The first is preliminary concentration (*parikammasamādhi*), which is produced as a result of the novice meditator's initial efforts to focus his mind on his meditation subject, The second is access concentration (*upacāra-samādhi*), marked by the suppression of the five hindrances, the manifestation of the *jhāna* factors, and the appearance of a luminous mental replica of the meditation object called the "counterpart sign" (*paṭibhāganimitta*). The third is absorption concentration (*appanāsamādhi*), the complete immersion of the mind in its object effected by the full maturation of the *jhāna* factors. Absorption concentration is equivalent to the eight attainments, the four *jhānas* and the four āruppas, and to this extent *jhāna* and *samādhi* coincide. However, *samādhi* still has a broader scope than *jhana*, since it includes not only the *jhānas* themselves but also the two preparatory degrees of concentration leading up to them. Further, *samādhi* also covers a still different type of concentration called "momentary concentration" (*khanikasamādhi*), the mobile mental stabilization produced in the course of insight-contemplation on the passing flow of phenomena.

Jhāna and the Constituents of Enlightenment

The principles of meditative training expounded by the Buddha during his teaching career were organized by him into seven basic categories comprising altogether thirty-seven *bodhi-pakkhiyā dhammā*, "states pertaining to enlightenment," The seven categories among which they are distributed are: the four foundations of mindfulness, the four right endeavors, the four bases of success, the five spiritual faculties, the five spiritual powers, the seven enlightenment factors, and the Noble Eightfold Path. The four *jhānas* enter either directly or implicitly into all these sets of training principles, and to appreciate their significance in the Buddhist discipline it will be of value to see how they do so. We will consider first the place of the *jhānas* in the Noble Eightfold Path, the most important and inclusive of the seven groups; then we will go on to note briefly their relation to the other sets.

The eight factors of the Noble Eightfold Path are right view, right intention, right speech, right action, right livelihood, right effort, right mindfulness, and right concentration. These eight are frequently divided into three broader categories: the group of moral discipline (*sīlakkhandha*), the group of concentration (*samādhikkhandha*), and the group of wisdom (*paññākkhandha*),[20] The group of moral discipline comprises the factors of right speech, right action, and right livelihood; the group of concentration the factors of right effort, right mindfulness, and right concentration; the group of wisdom the factors of right view and right intention. Though wisdom is seen as emerging fully only after concentration has been established its two factors are placed at the beginning of the path because a certain modicum of right understanding and right intentions are needed to embark upon the threefold discipline of morality, concentration and wisdom.

Of the three factors in the morality group, right speech is abstinence from false speech, slander, harsh speech, and idle talk; right action is abstinence from killing, stealing, and sexual misconduct; and right livelihood is avoiding a wrong means of earning one's living and following a righteous occupation. The Eightfold Path operates at the two levels previously referred to, at the mundane level in the preliminary stages of self-cultivation and at the supramundane level with the attainment of the four supramundane paths. This twofold modality of the path applies to each of its eight factors. The morality factors, considered in the Abhidhamma as three distinct mental concomitents, arise at the mundane level whenever a person deliberately abstains from some case of moral transgression. At the supramundane level the three factors occur simultaneously in the states of supramundane path-consciousness, performing the function of cutting off the tendencies towards their opposites.

The three factors of the concentration group also receive an analytical breakdown in the suttas. Right effort is explained as four right endeavors: the endeavor to prevent the arising of unarisen unwholesome mental state, to eliminate unwholesome states already arisen, to cultivate unarisen wholesome mental states, and to increase wholesome states already arisen. Right mindfulness consists in mindful contemplation of the four "foundations" of mindfulness" (satipaṭṭhāna) namely, the body, feelings, states of mind, and mental objects. Right concentration is the unification of the mind into one-pointedness through the four jhānas. At the supramundane level right effort becomes the energy factor in the paths and fruits, right mindfulness the factor of attention, and right concentration the factor of mental unification. As we will see, according to the Theravāda commentators concentration in the mundane portion of practice need not be developed to the degree of the four jhānas. However, because the stronger the degree of concentration the stabler the basis for insight, the jhānas are still commended as guaranteeing the most reliable groundwork of mental calm. And when the supramundance paths and fruits are attained, consciousness occurs with a force of absorption tantamount to the four (or five) jhānas. Thence the jhānas are included as components of the Noble Eightfold Path, entering via the group of concentration.

Concentration functions as a basis for wisdom. As the Buddha says: "Develop concentration; for one who has concentration understands things as they really are."[21] The wisdom group comprises the two factors of right view and right intention, the former being an equivalent term for wisdom proper, the latter its accompaniment. Right view is explained as the undistorted comprehension of the basic laws and truths structuring actuality. At the mundane level it consists in an understanding of the law of kamma, indicating the moral efficacy of action, as well as of the doctrinal contents of the Dhamma–the three characteristics, dependent arising, and the Four Noble Truths. At the supramundane level right view is the wisdom which directly penetrates the Four Noble Truths by "seeing" nibbāna, the unconditioned element. Right intention, its companion in this group, consists in thoughts of renunciation, of benevolence, and of non-injury. At the supramundane level right intention becomes the purified mental function free from lust, ill will, and cruelty, which fixes the mind upon nibbāna.

The three groups of path factors lock together as interrelated stages of training which work in harmony to accomplish the goal aspired to by the discipline, full liberation from suffering. From this angle the groups are designated the three trainings (*tisso sikkhā*). The morality group makes up the training in the higher morality (*adhisīla-sikkhā*), the concentration group the training in the higher consciousness (*adhicittasikkhā*), and the wisdom group the training in the higher consciousness (*adhipaññāsikkhā*).[22] Each of these trainings arises in dependence on its predecessor and provides the foundation for concentration, since mental composure can only be established when the coarser impulses towards ethical transgressions are controlled and restrained. Concentration provides the foundation for wisdom since clear perception of the true nature of phenomena requires the purification and unification of the mind. Wisdom reaches its climax in the four paths and fruits, which uproot the subtlest strata of defilements and issue in final liberation from suffering.

From the Noble Eightfold Path we can now turn briefly to the other groups to see how *jhāna* fits in with their constituents of enlightenment. The four foundations of mindfulness and the four right endeavors are identical, respectively, with right mindfuness and right effort of the Eightfold Path. Insofar as these are called the bases (*nimitta*) and requisites (*parikkhāra*) for concentration, and concentration includes the four *jhānas*, *jhāna* can be seen to arise from the training in these two groups of principles. The four bases of success are the base of success consisting in zeal, the base consisting in energy, the base consisting in connsciousness, and the base consisting in inquiry.[23] Since these four constituents of enlightenment are said to be supports for obtaining concentration, and to be directed towards the *abhiññās* and the supramundane attainments, their connection with the *jhānas* is evident.[24] The five faculties and powers comprise the five identical factors-faith, energy, mindfulness, concentration, and wisdom–[25] each classified as a faculty (*indriya*) in that they exercise dominance in a particular sphere of spiritual endeavor and as a power (*bala*) in that they cannot be shaken in confrontation with their opposites.[26] The faculty and power of concentration are said to be found in the four *jhānas*.[27] The seven enlightenment factors are mindfulness, investigation of phenomena, enrgy, rapture, tranquility, concentration, and equanimity.[28] *Jhāna* can be fitted into this group explicitly as the enlightenment factor of concentration; it is also closely associated with the factors of rapture, tranquility, and equanimity, which each rise to prominence in the course of developing the *jhānas*.

References

1. Digha Nikaya (PTS), 2 : 314-15; Majjhima Nikaya (PTS), I : 182.
2. Majjhima Nikaya (PTS), I : 246-47.
3. Ibid.
4. Digha Nikaya (PTS), 3 : 220.
5. Majjhima Nikaya, I : 68-83.
6. Digha Nikaya, 2 : 156.
7. Digha Nikaya, I:47-87, Majjhima Nikaya, I : 175-84, 256-80.
8. Anguttara Nikaya (PTS), 2 : 150-52.
9. Digha Nikaya, 2 : 131-32.
10. Ibid.
11. Samyutta Nikaya (PTS), 5 : 308.
12. Anguttara Nikaya, I : 116.
13. Ibid.
14. Ibid.
15. Majjhima Nikaya, I : 301.
16. Visuddhimagga (PTS), p. 84.
17. Ibid., p. 85.
18. Ibid., p. 68.
19. Narada, A Manual of Abhidhamma, Buddhist Publication Society, Kandy, 1980, pp. 389, 395-96.
20. Majjhima Nikaya, I : 301, 3 : 71-73; Digha Nikaya, 2 : 291-315.
21. Samyutta Nikaya, 3 : 13.
22. Anguttara Nikaya, I : 235-36.
23. Samyutta Nikaya, 5 : 249-93
24. Ibid., 5 : 268.

25. Ibid., 193-252.
26. Dhammapada, pp. 162-67.
27. Samyutta Nikāya, 5 : 196.
28. Ibid., 83-140.

13
Inter-Personal Relations And Vipassanā Meditation*

Professor Lily de Silva

The human being is essentially a social animal. He cannot survive alone.... The human child goes through a long period of growth before he can fend for himself in any meaninfgul way. During this period he needs the love and care of his parents. When he is older he needs the support of not only the members of his family but that of his community and society. Alone the human, being is defenceless and vulnerable, but together there seems to be hardly any problem he cannot surmount. As it is only by working together that man can lead a profitable meaningful life, interpersonal relations assume great significance in society.

Though essentially a social animal the human being practically lives alone in a private world of his own, constructed by his sense experience. No two human beings can share the same world of sense experience. Each one sees the world differently from his own perspective and each one reacts differently to what he sees too on his own unique way. What one person loves and treasures may be disliked and considered a trifle by another. What is beautiful and precious to one may be ugly and worthless to another. Thus each one of us has his own private world of sense experience with his own fears, guilts, prejudices, obsessions, likes and dislikes. This makes interpersonal relations problematic unless we understand

---

* New World Buddhism 2534 (1990), Colombo, Sri Lanka.

the realities underlying individual idiosyncrasies and adopt an intelligent sympathetic attitude of tolerance towards others.

When we deal with other people our relationships are influenced to a great extent by our previous experiences. Those who have generated feelings of pleasure and happiness in us we tend to regard as friends. Those who have generated painful feelings we tend to regard as enemies. Those who generate neutral feelings we regard as strangers. We hardly relate to others without any affective bias. Generally we have a mixture of these emotional biases when we relate to others. Similarly others too relate to us through emotional biases of their own making. As emotions generally distort reality and as they themselves keep on changing all the time, interpersonal relations which are coloured by them become complex and tricky, unpredictable and difficult. *Vipassana* meditation helps us a great deal to understand and master our emotions and thus improve the quality of our interpersonal relations.

The *Sigalovada Sutta*[1] enumerates six fundamental relationships an individual is called upon to enter into in society. They are the relationships between parents and, children, teachers and pupils, husband and wife, individual and friends employers and employees and the layman and the clergy. This *sutta* defines the mutual reciprocal duties and responsibilities of these societies and the stability and harmony of the relationship depends on the commitment of each member to his other duty. The rights of each member are duly fulfilled by the discharge of duties by other members in partnership. The neglect of duties causes the erosion of unity, quality of life and human values. The *sutta* seems to circumvent problems arising out of emotional biases and conflicts by laying emphasis on the moral obligations of each individual to other members of the society. The more closely one adheres to *sila*, moral precepts, the more harmonious these interpersonal relations become.

In the *Sakkapanha Sutta*[2] Sakka raises an interesting question regarding interpersonal relations. Though people wish and make pious resolutions to live in harmony with one another without enmity and aggregation, without recourse to weapons against one another, they in fact live in disharmony, harbouring anger and illwill against one another, sometimes resorting to, weapons to terrorise and kill one another. What is the reason for this paradoxical situation that in spite of wanting to live in harmony, they cannot do so? Buddha replies that unwholesome negative emotions such as jealousy, convetousness, likes and dislikes, partiality and pre-occupation with prejudices are responsible for intolerance, strife, disharmony and disunity in society.

The teaching of Buddha maintains that man's vision is obscured by five negative emotions called *nivarana* hindrances in Pali. These are the desire for sensual pleasures (*kamacchanda*), anger or illwill (*vyapada*), indolence and lethargy (*thinamiddha*), restlessness and worry (*uddhaccakukkucca*), and doubt or perplexity (*vicikiccha*)[3]. This group of five seems to summarise all man's negative emotions as practically all unwholesome emotions we can think of can be categorised under one or other in this group. For instance, greed and selfishness can be put under *kamacchanda*, jealousy, envy, hatred etc. under *vyapada*, indifference and callousness under *thinnamiddha*, pride and remorse under *uddhaccakukkucca*, and fear, anxiety and depression under *vicikiccha* etc. Thus the five *nivaranas* can be taken as quite a comprehensive analysis of negative emotions of man. Negative emotions cloud man's discerning ability and impair his judgemental capacities. This fact is beautifully illustrated by the simile of water in the *Bojjhanga samyutta*[4]. The mind over-powered by the desire for sensual pleasures is compared to coloured water which fails to give the true undiscoloured image of an object reflected on it. The mind over-powered by anger is compared to boiling water which also fails to reflect an image well. The lazy mind is compared to moss-covered water which is incapable of reflecting an image at all. The mind given to restlessness and worry is like wind-tossed turbulent water which cannot reflect a steady undisturbed image. The mind under the grip of doubt is like muddy water which cannot reflect a steady undisturbed image. The mind under the grip of doubt is like muddy water placed in darkness which also cannot portray a proper image. Thus the water simile is a lucid illustration of the inability of the mind to understand an issue in its realistic perspective when labouring under the weighty influence of negative emotions. When we are unable to judge issues impartially, problems get exaggerated far out of proportion and our interpersonal relations get adversely affected sometimes resulting in gruesome crimes and even widespread violence.

Emotions work in man at three interconnected levels and they are called in Pali *vitikkama, pariyutthana* and *anusaya*[5]. *Vitikama* is the overt level at which negative emotions burst into expression through the channels of verbal and physical behaviour. They may break social norms and codes of ethical behaviour. For instance if a man is under a spell of anger he will use abusive words and even resort to physical violence. When negative emotions assume such overt proportions interpersonal relations get disrupted or very much strained and impaired where negative emotions come to the surface of the mind, but do not find expression through words and deeds. For, instance, anger has arisen, but the person can restrain himself without giving vent to it verbally and physically. Here, though interpersonal relations may not get disrupted to the same extent as in the previous case, a sense of intolerance and an atmosphere of coldwar sets in. A person wont to experience this sort of 'boiling within' often, may become the victim of psychological and psychosomatic disorders. He is not at peace with himself. Depending on the intensity and frequency of these internal emotional experiences he can be at war with himself to a greater or lesser degree. He who is not peace with himself cannot have genuine peace with others around him. *Anusaya* is the latent level at which negative emotions lurk deep within the human mind. This is the melting pot of negative emotions where they get fermented. They constantly send emotional fumes and gases to the upper levels. This latent level is fed by negative reactions at the overt level. The more negative unethical behaviour is displayed at the verbal and the physical level the stronger the emotional fermentation at the latent level. The stronger the fermentation at the latent level the more prone the person becomes to violent behaviour at the overt level of words and deeds. Thus a vicious circle is formed. So long as this vicious circle is not broken so long the individual is at unrest or war with himself. So long as a person is a problem to himself so long he is a problem to society and interpersonal relations are at jeopardy.

Buddha's teaching prescribe a method of weakening this vicious circle and ultimately breaking it. The first step is to be restrained at the overt level by the observance of moral precepts (*sila*). An individual who refrains from negative antisocial behaviour through words and deeds prevents strengthening the latent level by feeding it with less and less emotional ammunition. At the social level he maintains respectable interpersonal relations. He would be a conscientious individual who meticulously discharges all his duties, such as those delineated in the *Sigalovadasutta*.

The conscious level of the manifestation of negative emotions is disciplined with tranquility meditation (*samathabhavana*). By this method the volatile mind is calmed and negative emotions are much weakened. The individual experiences peace proportionate to the calm he has developed. He also improves the quality of interpersonal relations to the same extent. The *Aghatavagga* of the Anuguttara Nikaya[6] explains how to deal with a specific negative emotion, namely anger which often besmears interpersonal relations. According to this discourse anger should be allayed considering the different character types of the people with whom one happens to get angry. The methods of consideration are illustrated with the help of appropriate similes. If a person gets angry with another who has blameworthy physical conduct but is blameless in verbal conduct, one must consider his good blameless verbal qualities and try to get rid of the anger. This is compared to taking the useful part of a rag and discarding the worn-out parts. If one gets angry with a person who has a foul mouth but is blameles in physical conduct, one must ignore his foul speech and appreciate his good physical conduct and thus try not to get angry. The simile given is of a pond covered with moss, where one can move aside the moss with one's hands and drink from the cool waters. Thus, turn a blind eye on his bad qualities and appreciate his good qualities and thereby get rid of the anger. If the person with whom one gets angry is evil in both verbal and physical behaviour, but displays good qualities from time to time, one must give credit to these rare moments of good conduct and not get angry with him.... It is like drinking water from a small puddle, taking care not to disturb its clear surface water. But if one gets angry with a person who has no good qualities at all, one must refrain from getting angry with him through pity. He should have compassion on him just as one would take pity and help a man who is desperately ill in a lonely desert. If, on the other hand, one happens to get angry with a person of pure noble qualities appreciate all his goodness and dispel the anger, just as one would drink, bathe and enjoy the cool waters of a large pollution free lake. Thus whatever the character of a person with whom one happens to get angry, one must try to get rid of the anger and restore a friendly wholesome relationship.

Anger is a dangerous negative emotion which defiles the mind and spoils interpersonal relations very quickly. It is compared to fire which burns its very support, as anger consumes the very person in whom it arises. The Visuddhimagga compares the act of trying to abuse another with anger to hitting another with live coal or excreta. It may or may not hit the target, but it certainly burns or defiles the hand that grabbed it. Thus the effect of anger is felt first by the person who generates it, it may or may not affect the person against whom it is directed. It can destroy harmony in interpersonal relations. Considering all these evils inherent in the negative emotion of anger, one must try to get rid of it. When anger is eliminated the mind gradually becomes filled with *metta*, loving kindness.

To improve the quality of interpersonal relations one can also practise the active cultivation of positive sublime emotions such as *metta, karuna, mudita,* and *upekkha* loving-kindness, compassion, sympathetic joy and equanimity, respectively. In order to practise these effectively one must understand what is meant by each. These are non-biological, non-utilitarian modes of human relationships which generate no sorrow or disappointment at any stage. *Metta* (Skt. *maitri*) is derived from *mitra* which means friend. Therefore its simplest meaning is friendliness. Pali commentators explain it as "the sublime emotion which softens and lubricates (the human heart) (*Mejjatiti metta, siniyhatiti attho*). It has to be carefully distinguished from *pema*, affection, which gives rise to grief (*Pemato jayati soko*). Compassion is the sublime emotion which impels one to help another in distress[10]. This has to be distinguished from personal involvement in others' troubles and the experience of sadness: it means the detached readiness to help. Sympathetic joy is the gladness one experiences in the happiness of another[11]. But this does not mean that one should develop a vested interest in another's success. Equanimity is the ability to maintain an even psychological balance in the face of the vicissitudes of life. These positive sublime emotions help a great deal to foster and cement harmonious interpersonal relations.

The meditation on loving-kindness (*mettabhavana*) is not confined to sitting quietly in a corner and repeating the phrase: "May all beings be well and happy". Repeating this phrase is one method of trying to impress this positive emotion into the mental make-up. One must do this repetition with deep sincerity and sensitivity so that it gets ingrained as a spontaneous emotion and a genuine attitude. In addition to this formalised exercise one must consciously cultivate *metta* in one's vocal and physical behaviour in dealing with others. Even a single word like "Yes" can be politely uttered to pour out *metta*, while a rude "Yes" can express anger and spoil an intimate relationship. When one is engaged in normal day-to-day activities too one can set about them calmly and gently with an attitude of amity and genuine interest in the work done. The same work can be done rudely in a haphazard manner with a display of negative emotions and that would deeply impair interpersonal relations. Therefore one intent on the cultivation of *metta* should take proper care of his verbal and physical behaviour as well. It is with the cultivation of *metta* that we can develop interpersonal relations free from emotional bias.

Even though the conscious level of negative emotions can be taken care of by these methods, the latent level of emotional fermentation can be eradicated only by the practice of insight meditation (*vipassanabhavana*). This stops the surge of negative emotions from deep within to the conscious and overt levels and the individual begins to experience deeply satisfying peace within himself. His peace remains undisturbed even when provoked. It is such a person who is capable of establishing genuinely harmonious interpersonal relations.

Let us now consider the practical aspect of *Vipassana* meditation. Generally *vipassana* cannot be practised without a basis of tranquility (*samatha*). Tranquility is best, developed with *anapanasati*, the awareness of the inbreath. There is nothing mysterious or mystical about this practice, it is an exercise to calm the monkeylike restless mind. When the mind gradually calms down with the regular practice of *samatha* one begins to *notice* the appearance of negative emotions whenever they occur. This is a great step forward as one was not even aware of the appearance of negative emotions earlier. It is true for instance, that one has reacted to anger with impolite behaviour on many an occasion, but it is done mechanically, unmindfully. That is why one cannot often remember what one said or did at a moment of intense hostility. To be *aware* of the fact that one is angry is itself a meditative experience. The second step is the mastery of anger is to restrain oneself from giving vent to anger verbally or physically *being aware of the fact* that one is restraining one's negative behaviour. When this has been repeated on a number of occasions (and the *anapanasati* exercise is going on regularly) one begins to notice the physical sensations one experiences at the time one is angry. These sensations comprise feeling hot, breaking out in a sweat, faster heartbeat, restlessness, and so on. When one pays attention to these physical manifestations corresponding to the emotion of anger, one will be surprised to note how anger itself subsides. When this process is repeated on a number of occasions when anger is present, gradually anger diminishes in intensity as well as frequency. One gradually begins to notice a transformation in one's character. An impatient, irritable person becomes a tolerant, amiable person. Positive sublime emotions such as loving kindness, compassion, sympathetic joy and equanimity begin to emerge. One begins to experience peace within, and peace in all interpersonal relationships. Thus it is by the practice of *Vipassana* meditation at the inidividual level that genuine lasting peace can be fostered at social level. When peace at individual level is widespread the social fabric gets woven into a beautiful pattern of high quality culture elegantly embroidered with the peace and harmony of interpersonal relations.

References

All references are to Pāli Text Society editions

1. Dīghanikāya III 190 ff.
2. ibid II 276.
3. ibid I 71.
4. Saṁyuttanikāya V 121-125.
5. Visuddhimagga I 5.
6. Aṅguttaranikāya III 186-190.
7. Visuddhimagga I 301.
8. Atthasālinī 192
9. Dhammapada 213.
10. Atthasālinī 192.
11. ibid 193.

14
Vipassanā Meditation And Its Application In Social Change*

Pravinchandra S. Shah

What Vipassanā Meditation Is?

Vipassanā means to see things as they are; to see things in their true perspective, in their true nature. Vipassanā is an art of living. It is a technique of self-observation, truth observation and self-exploration by oneself only. Vipassanā frees the individual from all the negativities of Mind such as anger, greed, ignorance. It works for happiness of one and all in the society. Vipassanā means total liberation and full enlightenment. Craving, aversion and ignorance - the roots of unhappiness - are uprooted by Vipassanā and an individual is totally HAPPY, LIBERATED with full enlightenment. It means self-introspection. It is a search for the Eternal Truth within oneself.

Vipassanā is a process of awakening one's own Mind and thereby achieving automatic self-control. It is a cure of all mind illusions and fantasies. It is the normaliser of our nature, the cleanser of our mental garbage so as to establish one in one's SAHAJA (Normal) compassionate, loving being. It is pure awareness without any intruding thoughts. It is a way to freedom from Births and Deaths. It is an eternal peace which is Real - True Happiness. Vipassanā keeps one aware of *ANICCA* (impermanence) and so

---

* The Seminar on Vipassana Meditation, Vipassana Reseach Institute, Igatpuri, Maharashtra, India. December 1986.

of *Dukkha* (Sufferings) and *Anattā* (Egolessness) - which is the secret of success. It works for one's salvation with diligence. Observation of *Law of Impermanence* is the essence of Vipassanā and when one lives observing this Law, suffering goes - vanishes; as a result, Egolessness - ultimate truth prevails. Vipassanā is a knowing - experience and not knowledge - theory. It is LOVE and not logic. It is Heart and not Head. When impermanence (*ANICCA*) is experienced and understood by practice through the technique of Vipassanā, all the defilements of Mind (good-bad; like-dislike; craving-aversion; etc.) vanish till one is liberated of all *"SANKHĀRAS"* (formations). Vipassanā is a study - process - practice of *Sīla, Samādhi* and *Paññā;* i.e., insight meditation. It is choiceless, effortless awareness and its practice keeps one aware - awake of Natural Law of Impermanence which is inherent nature of everything that exists in the Universe - whether animate or inanimate.

When Vipassanā Meditation begins "ME ends", "PAST and FUTURE cease", "all divisions drop", "Existence is experienced." It is a state of No Mind - *"SHUNYATA."* It is an art of "LET GO" in life. Vipassanā Meditation is free from clutches of time and space and there is harmony between thought, work and action. The practice of Vipassanā shows truth in its nakedness. It is light in darkness. As a blind person after cornea grafting gets sight and feels happy, similarly one gets light of knowing - experience free from thoughts - theory, which is *"SAMYAK-DARSHAN"* - *"STHITA-PANNATĀ"* - *"BLISS"* - *"ENLIGHTENMENT",* etc. As Vipassanā Meditation practice grows, inner richness enhances and sphere of Love and Compassion increases in all dimensions of life. When one observes things as they are, and when one observes sensations of the body as they are, one starts getting liberated of all *'SANKHĀRAS'.*

Vipassanā Meditation is just sitting and doing nothing. Its experience can never be written in words since it is the experience of REAL HAPPINESS. Only the path can be shown where one has to work for oneself only. Though the main purpose of this meditation is total liberation of all the *SANKHĀRAS,* yet as a by-product physical - psychosomatic diseases are eradicated, tensions released and tied knots of old habits of reacting to pleasant and unpleasant situations are opened up soon. Vipassanā Meditation aims at the highest spiritual goals of total liberation and full enlightenment. Its purpose is not the curing of physical disease, but as a by-product of mental purification, many psychosomatic diseases are eradicated. Actually, Vipassanā eliminates the three causes of all unhappiness - craving, aversion and ignorance. With continued practice, the meditation releases the tensions developed in everyday life and opens the knots tied by the old habit of reacting in an unbalanaced way to pleasant and unpleasant situations.

What Vipassanā Meditation is Not :

It is not a rite or ritual based on blind faith. It is neither an intellectual nor philosophical entertainment. It is not a rest cure, a holiday or opportunity for socialising. It is not an escape from the trials and tribulations of everyday life nor an asylum for disgruntled misfits. It is not memory - visualisation or future plans. It is not going into PAST or FUTURE but being Alert - Awake and Equanimous in present circumstances. It promotes sound Mental Health since Vipassanā is neither hold-on nor clinging to people, events, insults, injuries, etc.

Its Application in Social Change :

(a) Induction of Human Values :

Vipassanā Meditation has a great impact upon one's mind and relaxation of Mental Health is gained thereby. The root of all the diseases is unequanimous mind, which is cured by Vipassanā Meditation. The Medical Science of the day has also recognised the importance of equanimous mind which is a product of Vipassanā Meditation. People suffering from any disease slowly may practise Vipassanā which will help to have speedy recovery. Health problems can be solved by this meditation. A number of Vipassanā meditators have cured their diseases such as Hypertension, Pain, Glands Subsiding. Many Cardiologists advise Vipassanā Meditation for lower cardio-respiratory rate and for elevated blood pressure patients. It is proved that Meditation is of far greater importance than Medication.

On physical level, it helps each cell to revitalise itself; it facilitates digestion; it makes respiration more efficient; it improves circulation and quality of blood.

On mental level, it becomes a methodology to train the mind to concentrate; it cleans and relaxes the mind; it offers a way to treat serious psychosomatic illnesses without drugs; it is an efficient exercise in self-discipline leading to the end of addiction and other bad habits; it leads to what lies beyond conscious mind.

On emotional level, the active functioning of reasoning mind controls reactions to environmental conditions, situations and behaviour of others; harmonization of the functioning of nervous and endocrine systems results in control and ultimate eradication of fear, hatred, jealousy, anger, lust and sexual perversion.

On spiritual level, the firm control of the reasoning mind, regulation and transformation of blood chemistry through proper blending of the neuro-endocrinal secretions and production of dispassionate internal vibrations leads to attain infinite compassion, equanimity, bliss and happiness.

The habits of an individual can be changed for the better by the practice of Vipassanā meditation. The mental nature of a criminal can also be changed to a fully civilized one. Since Vipassanā is a cure of tensions of mind, one can be made capable of handling more work, getting better results, etc. In the past, courses were held in jails, temples and mosques with very good results.

The relations amongst the members of the family, staff members of the office, workers of the factory, etc. are straightened out in-between the people and cordial relations are established. Vipassanā meditation does not have an impact only on meditators but also upon others who come in contact of these persons. The obvious reasons are, the vibrations generated by the Vipassanā meditators inspire others for cordial happy relations and the harmony is maintained in family, office and factory, due to Vipassanā Meditation. Vipassanā Meditation generates love and compassion in place of ill-will and hatred and there are many examples in past and present, as reported in "Vipassanā Patrika" by a number of meditators.

Vipassanā Meditation releases a person from drugs and intoxicants, drinks and smoking, etc. and greater awareness of one's duty towards the society is inculcated. Even the efficiency level is increased to a considerable extent in spheres of work.

(b) Fostering National Integration :

Vipassanā meditation is very helpful in fostering National Integration. A nation is made of individuals and an individual is treated with love and compassion in Vipassanā meditation. One is trained to improve oneself not by exhortation of moral precepts but by instilling in one the desire to change. One is taught to explore oneself and generate a process which brings about the change and leads to purification of mind. Such a change from individual to individual of any nation will help National Integration.

Vipassanā is taught without any consideration of class, colour or creed. It is real-basic education and not so-called religion. When the nation is divided amongst a number of religions, number of languages and number of rites and rituals, Vipassanā Meditation works to foster National Integration. The technique of Vipassanā Meditation is totally universal since it is a remedy to the universal disease of craving and aversion. The Vipassanā Meditation can be practised by one and all without any division of vocations and thus foster National Integration. It is helpful in opening of knots tied over in the past by one against another following different vocations, religions and languages. Vipassanā meditators do not count themselves in terms of being or belonging to a particular religion, community, language or vocation. They are trained at par with others, taking human values and no prominence is given to the outer rites, rituals and dogmas which create divisions among the people. They are taught to live happily with others at the time of training and the same habit is being followed by them in their field of life after Vipassanā course. Even the children learning Vipassanā Meditation widen their limits of mind sphere and there is wide scope of national integration when they become grown-up citizens. All the barriers in the way of non-integration such as rites, rituals, languages, dress, etc. are not given any prominence in Vipassanā Meditation practice and as a result, all communities can live in harmony. The impact of Vipassanā Meditation is very high to have national integration. The disease of craving and aversion, greed and lust, likes and dislikes, pleasants and unpleasants, etc. is not sectarian and hence the remedy cannot be sectarian and it must be universal. Everyone faces the problem of suffering, whether one is a Hindu, Christian, Jain or Buddhist. Therefore, Vipassanā Meditation which has proved to be a universal remedy for all maladies, the practice - preaching of Vipassanā Meditation will foster National Integration to a greater extent. Central Government and State Governments should come forward to give more and more help in this task of practising and preaching of Vipassanā Meditation; the Governments will be able to solve their problem of drugs and intoxicants. Thus, a number of national problems can be solved as a result through Vipassanā Meditation and foster National Integration.

(c) Strengthening Secularism :

India is a secular State and it is the need of the hour to strengthen secularism. Vipassanā Meditation is a 'must' for one and all. It is a real education to live and let live happily. The problems of life are alike to all the people and as such Vipassanā Meditation which is a basic education to strengthen secularism should be well propagated and practised by any nation which avows to strengthen its ideal of secularism. Indian nationals are divided into many castes, religions, languages and to strengthen secularism Vipassanā Meditation will work miracles. The obvious reasons are - state of mind is cleaned, divisions are dropped and the love and compassion is increased by Vipassanā Meditation. This Meditation deals with human psyche and one who practises it easily changes one's attitude and perceptions. The people can come out of bad habits in temperament, behaviour and relationships.

Vipassanā Meditation is a study for an individual and one is filled with love and compassion, which ultimately passes on to other members of society. This strengthens national secularism. Fights between members of same caste, same religion and same language are brought to a stop since Vipassanā meditator is above all these divisions. His mind is purified and enriched by Vipassanā Meditation. Such a change will be lasting and enduring. Many Vipassanā meditators have put forth the changes they have found in them after practice in feeling of fellowship with others and thus strengthen secularism in India. Social change from outside is not lasting. Laws compelling changes do not last long. There is a fundamental change from the root of one's concept by Vipassanā Meditation since it takes one to the root-cause of all the problems. It is to know things as they are at the root of problems and as a result problems at the national level can be solved and thus strengthen secularism by Vipassanā Meditation practice.

15

How To Overcome Restlessness Through Vipassanā*

Kusuma Devendra

What is Restlessness?

We can describe restlessness as a condition of mind generally manifested by a lack of satisfaction. On careful observation we see that it is a condition arising out of our lack of awareness of the present moment. The mind is most of the time dwelling on the past or on the future, and appears to flit from one thing to another in an unidentified hurry. We are thus constantly preoccupied and are for ever involved in thinking, planning, imagining, doubting, blaming, and weighing and thus often rushing into conclusions. In addition, restlessness may sometimes be manifest as a lack of memory. Restlessness is seen when speaking and behaving without thinking. When the same thought occurs over and over again without control, we become restless. Excessive restlessness can even cause madness, and halucinations. Hence it may be summarised that the overall effect of restlessness is the inability of the mind to concentrate on any one thing for a period of time.

What is the cause of restlessness?

In Buddhist texts the cause of restlessness is attributed to the constant recurrance of unskilful thoughts. Every time an impression arrives at the sense doors or at the mind door, it tends

* The Maha Bodhi, Volume 97, July-September 1989, pp. 50-55.

to generate a train of thoughts. This is true even to the supreme Buddha and the Saints. But it is the interpretation of these impressions which become skilful or unskilful. In the case of the ordinary beings or puthuijanas, due to the prevalence of restlessness, and (ignorance) the interpretations are often un-skilful. There are about twelve main thought processes identified and categorised in the Buddhist texts, which are unskilful, and these thoughts occuring frequently account for the state of restlessness in the mind. They are—

(1) Attachment (lobha)
(2) Anger or aversion
(3) Ignorance
(4) Wrong view
(5) Pride
(6) Jealousy
(7) Stinginess or self pity
(8) Doubt
(9) Shamelessness regarding morals
(10) Lack of moral dread
(11) Sloth and Torpor
(12) Remorse.

Let us peruse these thought processes closely. We will recognise at once that all these tend to really harm us and others by generating a vacillating and restless mind. These thoughts have their effect directly on speech and other bodily actions. We shall now briefly discuss each of these mental states.

Attachment :

Except the peerless Buddha and the Arihants all other beings are attached to various things in various ways at all times of the day. These could be persons or things, food or music or any kind of pleasant mental state. If a person is not careful and is not sensible, these thoughts could easily become a source of noticeable restlessness. There are two ways in which attachment can cause restlessness. Firstly, restlessness is caused when a person constantly attempts to achieve or maintain only "good things" and to eschew unhappy situations. Secondly since all phenomena good or evil are subject to the inexorable law of change, the attempt to maintain and continue only "good things" causes restlessness. This process is going on morning, noon and night in the minds of those beings who are indulging in the quest for material comforts. They are so enraptured by this quest that they cannot pause to think whether it is necessary or even possible to live without them. But considering the dangers that can accrue to this life and the next, it is very necessary to reduce attachments to a minimum. Therefore it is necessary that a person must learn to relax and to derive satisfaction from all the little pleasures one gets from simple living This can be achieved by living in the present moment, rather than recount past experiences or hope for a brighter future, by fostering unconscious urges to require greater and more powerful attachments. This conscientious attempt to live only in the present moment will lead a person towards insightful meditation and thus to the gradual annihilation of restlessness.

Anger or aversion :

Here a person has only got to analyse one of his past moments of anger to vividly recall, how anger generates very insistent symptoms of restlessness. Sometimes this restlessness gets so uncotrollable and violent that it even leads to bodily agitation and violent action as well. Fortunately it is easier to recognise the symptoms of anger which are very gross unlike attachment which is quite subtle. Since manifest painful sensations occur during anger, it is easily recognised and noticed at its very inception. If this ability to notice anger is conscientiously developed a person can control this frightful tendency.

Ignorance :

This unskilful mental process is manifest in all puthujjanas and it clouds his vision and drives him to think and act in terms of the belief in the existence of an "I" and "mine". Such a person will instinctively order his way of life to preserve and develop this entity called 'I'. In fact, all unskilful mental states are the result of this overpowering ignorance. Ignorance can be dispelled by trying to see reality using the method of insight meditation.

Insight meditation aims at giving us the greatest freedom by making it possible for us to penetrate reality and to understand that there is no such permanent self as 'I' but that a being in a mirage resulting from Kamma producing thoughts. This is the doctrine of "Anatta" and the crux of the immaculate Buddha's teaching. Anatta means a lack of ownership of any description. One can easily grasp the intellectual aspect of the Anatta doctrine when one realises that even one's supposed body is ephemeral and does not belong to one. This body of ours becomes sick and old and dies much against our will and desire. This clearly shows that the body is beyond our control. Our mind also becomes angry and frustrated and sad, much against our will. This shows that the mind is also beyond our control. If the body and mind are our own, we should be able to control and command it at will. This is what we mean by a lack of ownership. When our body itself cannot be controlled by us, how can we control nature, things and other persons? We only appear to do so, for a short period of time. In the ultimate sense it cannot be done. Man may pass laws and by-laws, but the so called "Our property" is at all times common property to robbers and kings, ants and rats, bacteria and climate, circumstances and accidents, death and disease. Our pleasures and our life itself can be robbed by any one of those (or many others), regardless of any sense of reason or time or place.

Where is the ownership? This is the exact circumstance in which we exist. This knowledge is called 'Yatha Bhutha Nana', or realisation through insight meditation. This realisation may come as a challenge and a wholesome shock to our age old acceptances, loves and hates, etc. But it stands out firmly fearlessly typical of truth and actuality. It is as if the results of research or a scientist. This insight knowledge when experienced through correct meditative practice, does not depress or elate but only makes one look at life with equanimity and poise and understand the activity of the senses and their mental repercussion in the way of Karmic formations. When one experiences the idea that there is no self, all "values" break down. But a sense of ease and calm and an utter lack of restlessness pervades the being. The final liberation is the undisturbed rhythm of the mind of the saint. But all those who take to meditation will realise various degrees of temporary calm and ease while engaged in meditative reflections at a very early stage of practice. This is because the idea of 'I' and 'Mine' is abandoned temporarily. This pleasant experience will give the necessary incentive to forge ahead.

Wrong View :

We will very briefly try to understand the 4th kind of unskilful thought, i.e. wrong view, Very often we are quite unaware that we are holding a wrong view at all. And what is more, even if we are aware, our prejudices and prides and jealousies sustain and support our wrong view. The ordinary person makes judgements hastily without viewing the situation in all its complexity, giving due reference to the context, and the past and the future. Hence the ordinary man's views are bound to be only fragmentarily or comparatively correct and certainly not absolutely correct. This is because we cannot see objectively and impersonally due to self interest, which creeps in without our knowledge. They are only the peerless Buddhas and the saints who are able to judge and estimate without any prejudice or self interest. So, we must realise that all our views and assertions are partly true. Holding to these wrong views stubbornly is an ideal condition for all the other kinds of unskilful thoughts to arise. We must realise that what we can grasp with our senses are infinitesimal and what we cannot grasp with our senses is infinite. Hence our views are bound to be slight and superficial and these can harm us to a very great degree.

Pride, Jealousy, Stinginess:

Pride, Jealousy, Stinginess-are easy to recognise in one's self as well as in others. The meditative mind merely observes these thoughts objectively without becoming perturbed, frightened, or disgusted. It is then easy to notice the moments when these have arisen or when they have passed away. Meditation is a strictly mental process, there is no place for verbal or physical comment of any kind. Observing the arising of various thought processes should be the main concern of the meditator all throughout the day even while engaged in day to day activities. As the practice develops it becomes very easy to quickly stifle any unskilful thought and bring about mind control. This kind of mind control is not a repression because, in repression a person substitutes some other thoughts for the unpleasant ones formed and thus, the unwholesome thought is shelved for a moment to rise again when conditions are favourable. This is what the ordinary man resorts to, most of the time, being unaware of a better method using meditation. The observing mind in meditation recognises unskillful thoughts at a very early stage of occurence, and once recognised it vanishes, since the intervening recognition thought is a wholesome thought. Thus the evil chain is ruptured, and restlessness is not developed. One has to develop and practise mindfulness constantly, otherwise one may fall into lapses as this is the habit of worldlings. But the beginner should not be deterred. Constant and regular application to ever new situations in the course of the day is the one and only method to gain ultimate success in meditation.

Doubt:

An ordinary person often considers doubt as a sign of wisdom. This is manifest among learned people who want proof to accept anything. In Buddhist concepts doubt is an unskilful state of mind, and one should make every effort to get rid of it : as soon as possible by reading books or questioning more knowledgeable persons, or thinking out clearly and honestly. The human mind is limited and it is only through meditative practice that the mind gains insight to see things as they really are, and it is only then that all traces of doubt will be dispelled. Hence for a start a person has to place his faith on the Buddha, Dhamma and Sangha and accept certain tenets until he is able thereby to gain his own wisdom. If not, it becomes a terrible, obsession with most educated people who become doubtful of every conceivable idea, and in this way a whole life time could be wasted by constant vacillation.

Lack of Moral Shame and Lack of Moral Dread :

Lack of moral shame and Lack of moral dread-makes a person worthless however educated, rich or powerful he may be, because he descends to the low level of animals. In fact it is mainly these two factors that tend to draw the distinction between men and animals. In Buddhist countries the practice of observing the precepts is seen as a voluntary acceptance. It is not in the nature of submitting to an order. In fact the prcepts are worded as follows in order to emphasise its nature of non-compulsion, namely; 'I undertake the rule of training to refrain from destroying life....stealing, sexual misconduct, lying and indulging in intoxicants. If these precepts are adhered to from the very young days, it leads a person to develop a good moral conduct and shields a person from the shame and dread of immoral acts and consequent restlessness.

Sloth and Torpor :

Sloth and torpor make the mind inert and utterly unsuitable for any sustained thinking or deep contemplation. This condition is also conducive to restlessness, in that it does not allow the mind to remain for any length of time on any one object (arammana). It is the opposite of being overtly active.

Remorse:

In Buddhist literature, remorse is also a kind of unskillful thought. One should not recall again and again the wrong that one has done or any good that one has failed to do. The constant harking back to the past does not help a person to progress. It only tends to generate sorrow or remorse, since the good cannot be reproduced or the evil be cancelled.

Thus, we have briefly described the unwholesome factors that lead to restlessness and consequent unhappiness. The Compassionate Buddha has indicated a simple way to over-come these obstacles that beset a normal being in his daily life, and that is to develop insight meditation.

How to practise Insight Meditation :

At the very outset it must be mentioned that the best method would be to follow a two or three weeks practice in a residential meditation centre, such as the one found at Kanduboda, in Srilanka. If this is not possible one can make a start in one's home and office or working place-while engaged in ordinary day to day activities. There are many ways of doing this and one must try one or many of these methods, until one is firmly established in mindfulness. Mindfulness takes away unskilful thoughts and along with it restlessness also disappears. The idea is to tie the mind down to the present activity at hand and not allow the mind to flit into the past or future. Some Methods to practice Insight Meditation:

(1) Awareness : In insight meditation we begin to concentrate deeply on sense impressions. Such impressions coming through any one of the six sense doors are cognised separately, but the meditator will, to begin with, see as if all impressions occur simultaneously. This is because the speed of thought is so great that a whole train of thoughts pass off as one thought. With the development of meditation a person is able to observe these different sense impressions as they occur and to recognise their arising as well as their passing away. This must be noticed at all times of the day, while working or resting.

(2) Substitution of the opposite tendency; This method is difficult for it consists of nullifying an unwholesome thought process by the opposite wholesome thought process. For instance, when anger arises, one becomes immediately aware of anger and then conscientiously generates thoughts of non-anger towards that person or circumstance causing the anger. Similarly thoughts of selfishness are immediately countered by thoughts of generosity, thoughts of immorality by thoughts of morality etc. By this effort, one becomes quite adept in squashing all unskilful tendencies almost at their inception and developing skilful tendencies. Such a person is assured of a contended life, unruffled by the eight worldly factors (Ashtha Loka Dharma).

(3) Observing Postures : In this method a person takes notice of one's postures, be it standing, sitting, walking, or lying down, just

observing these postures right through the day as mere impersonal processes of the mind (nama) and body (rupa) one begins to realise that all these activities however small or great have to be willed by the mind, and that there is no automatic activity, In fact, the realisation dawns that it is nama and rupa together that create skilful and unskilful actions, that establishes Karmic bondage. Apart from nama and rupa there is no 'I' that acts–it is easy to describe this method, but it is difficult to be constantly applying it during a working day because of the lack of mind-fulness during most of our actions. All that has to be done is, while sitting just be aware of the posture of sitting, while walking, just be aware of walking, etc, without thinking of anything else.

(4) Observing Sense Objects : One can observe sights, sounds, smells, tastes and tactile stimuli as mere impersonal physical processes, i.e. rupa and observe the mental processes of seeing, hearing, smelling, tasting and bodily feeling and thinking as mental processes, nama. Looking at the world again and again in this way, establishes the understanding that there is no 'I' apart from nama and rupa, and that nama and rupa are indifferent, independent, inpersonal processes which arise and fall away due to certain conditions. The conceptual thinking about nama and rupa is not direct experiencing. It is the constant meditative observation in different situations what is necessary. In reality rupa or physical phenomena defy any kind of description. They are devoid of colour, shape, depth, name, sound, smell or taste or value. They are only sensory perceptions occuring at the site of the sense doors arising due to contact of the sense base with an external object. Rupa can be experienced only in this way. The multiplicity of the individual components and this rapidity of the attendent thought processes gives the illusion of a thing or self. It is this self idea that must be eradicated. Mental phenomena too gives the illusion of a continuity, which are then misunderstood and labelled as 'my thoughts', thereby propagating the concept of a self that thinks. The concept of self can be eradicated only if one develops the wisdom which clearly shows that all phenomena in us and around us are only nama and rupa and nothing else but nama and rupa.

(5) Meditating upon the loathsomeness of the body : It is an excellent method to contemplate on the loathesomeness of the body, which is for ever exuding unpleasant excretions from the various orifices. As soon as the bad smell, colour texture of the body matter is felt either in connection with one's body or of another person's one must remember that the body is extremely unclean both in the outside, and inside and it needs constant cleaning with soap and water, and application of scents and powders. This meditation takes away the senseless intoxication for life and its pleasures. This helps to dispell the attachment to the self and to direct one to a more sustained meditation.

(6) Awareness of Death : That death may occur at any moment must be contemplated as often as possible. In fact, a person must realise that death is lurking everywhere whether in a house or in the open or in a vehicle etc. This will take off all prides and prejudices as well as a host of their unskilful thoughts and gives an urgency to forge ahead towards complete eradication of the causes for death and suffering.

(7) Contemplation on the supreme Buddha : This meditation consists of contemplating on the superlative qualities of the peerless Buddha. Whenever one is subject to an unwholesome thought, one should immediately recall the fact that the supreme Buddha never entertained such thoughts, and seek solace in relinquishing those unwholesome thoughts. This constant awareness of the excellent qualities of the Buddha will help not only bringing in joy and rapture but also tend to bring in mental equanimity, poise and protection.

In this article a brief attempt has been made to indicate some of the ways in which one of the major defiling factors common to all laymen, namely, restlessness arises and then some meditative practices are described in order to show how this defilement can be overcome.

Buddhism is a way of life. It is not running away from life. It can be practised here and now amidst life's troubles and tribulations. The superlative Buddha has emphatically stated the "One way" (Ekayano Maggo) to salvation is mindfulness. Hence may all beings strive to gain inner peace and comfort through meditation.

May all beings be well and happy.

16
A Step Towards Happiness*
(Vipassanā Meditation)

Mathieu Boisvert

In this world of perpetual movement, suffering forever shakes the hearts of all beings. Each moment, thousands of beings encounter death, either from war, theft, or disease; millions of animals are slaughtered, either for the satisfaction of man's hunger for his own pleasure or for other selfish ends. Uncountable are the number of people suffering and decaying in the hospitals and the asylums; unnumbered are the crippled, the orphans, the starvelings. In the society where we live, we cannot keep track of all the rapes, divorces, murders and suicides. Suffering is part of life, yet behind all this gross, manifest suffering there is a suffering which lies inside each of us : the suffering of insatiable desire.

From the time one wakes in the morning until the time one goes to bed, one keeps on ranning here and there, doing things without quite knowing why jumping from one pleasure to another without ever being satisfied. Life begins with a cry, grows in the shadow of fear, and in the end is swept away by death. Each moment of our life is an attempt to escape from the present. In fulfilling our life of pleasures, we do not lessen suffering; we hide reality, suppress the truth beneath a world of illusions.

When a desire enters our mind, we invest all our energy in realizing it. We think of nothing else and when it is fulfilled, we cannot even appreciate it because our mind is already "en route"

---

* The Maha Bodhi, Calcutta, January-March 1986, pp. 9-18.

towards the conquest of another desire. This is how the mind has been conditioned. It cannot refrain from desiring, from being "en route" towards a goal. Our first priority, personal happiness, evades us because our conditioning induces us to postpone true satisfaction until tomorrow: "I will be happy only when I have achieved this..." The cycle is interminable. Once the seed of desire is sown, it germinates, grows into a big tree bearing hundreds of fruits, each of which contains another seed of desire that will grow again according to the same pattern–an endless process.

If one continues to believe that sensual pleasure is the only way to find happiness, he will definitely become entangled in suffering because all sensual pleasures have a common characteristic from which the suffering arises; *Impermanence*. No pleasure can last eternally. And even if it seems to last, the one who enjoys it will eventually pass away and this will put an end to the pleasure. This is the Law of nature: nothing is eternal, everything that is born must wither and die.

During the fulfilment of a desire, we can be happy for the period of time that the pleasure lasts, but as soon as it is over, we miss it and fall back even lower in our misery with the need to fulfil the next desire that has arisen in the mind. It is impossible to enter into the race for pleasure without encountering misery. There is no pleasure without pain: they are two faces of the same coin.

Attachment to a desire reinforces the craving and makes for even greater suffering than the original desire itself. Attachment is the dep-rooted cause of all our misery, and all the defilements of the mind (craving, aversion, hatred, animosity, ill-will) sooner or later beget attachment. Attachment is not only limited to our physical structure but also to our opinions and ideas. What could be the cause of conflicts, of war? Two different persons have their own perception of the world; they are so attached to their own visions that they cannot understand someone who thinks differently. Two nations become involved in war mostly because of the clinging to their own views, their own ego, their desires, their rites and rituals. We all see reality through the coloured glasses of our past conditioning. Because each one of us sees a different colour, we cannot find agreement. It is only when we take off those glasses of attachment that we see reality as it is : impermanent and constantly changing. Only then we come to a common agreement. Only then we can understand that our clinging to the people, things and ideas that we like is bound to bring suffering because all that we are attached to will never stay as it is. Impermanence is inherent in everything.

Although we know perfectly well that our desires constantly give birth to a lot of pain, dissatisfaction and unhappiness, like drug addicts who cannot end their addiction despite their knowledge of the risks, we find it difficult to master addiction to pleasures. Where can we find the key that will enable us to conquer the craving and aversion which keep us so agitated, so unhappy? What is the secret to achieving balance of mind amidst the fluctuation of worldly life?

Different Ways

In his search for happiness beyond pleasures of the senses and material possessions man has devised numerous techniques of spiritual practice. A brief glance at some of these may help us find the key for which we are searching.

One such spiritual technique is devotion which is usually directed to a deity or saintly person. Devotion is a very good attitude to develop, but it is often wrongly understood. Sometimes a devotee identifies himself with a particular sect or religion and refuses to consider those outside this sect to be proper persons. This kind of devotion creates a tremendous amount of attachment within one-self and friction with others. Sometimes, devotees feel that their devotion is sufficient to guarantee their salvation, and feel free to neglect all[2] moral standards in their belief in the unfailing presence of divine grace. This is blind devotion. A *real* devotee will continually try to develop the qualities representing the divinity or the saintly person he admires. The devotee of Jesus will try to develop boundless love for everyone, the devotee of the Buddha will try to develop infinite compassion and equanimity, to keep balance of his mind in every situation of life.

When a defilement arises in the mind to overcome it, some devotees divert their mind from it by imagining the picture of their God or saint. Thus it seems that the defilement goes away. This technique removes the defilement at the surface level of the mind but at a deeper level, in the subconscious, it still remains, for it has not been eradicated at the root, but only suppressed. The seed of that particular defilement is still growing deep in the unconscious and, if not checked and destroyed, may eventually turn into many bitter fruits. Devotion is essential to our search for happiness, but even right devotion is not sufficient. Right devotion is the first step we have to take on the path, so we can get inspired to develop good qualities, but it cannot give us the way to get rid of deep rooted attachment nor to develop those good qualities.

Another technique quite popular nowadays is the repetition of a certain sacred word called a mantra, for example; Om, or the name of the God we are devoted to. Each mantra has its own particular vibration and when we keep on repeating it our body is engulfed in this vibration and our minds become highly concentrated. When we are concentrated in this manner, we do not suffer because we are not aware of what is happening around and within ourselves. It is like running away from pain, like closing our eyes to suffering and as we know, suffering can often be more harmful if it is suppressed than if it is openly confronted and recognized. What is the good of high concentration if it does not lead to the true eradication of attachment, the cause of suffering. Concentration is essential to overcome suffering, but it must be *right* concentration directed to the extinction of defilements.

Another spiritual approach is an elementary philosophy based on the harmony of two principles; Yin and Yang (male and female, positive and negative). Yin and Yang are principles innate to everything in the universe. Something is either more Yin or more Yang combined to something else. The people who believe this philosophy of complementary opposites think that if we eat balanced food (where the two principles are harmonized) our body will automatically become harmonized. This seems cogent because the food taken into the body is bound to have some effect on the quality of consciousness, but these people seem to forget that the mind also has its own independent input: the mental defilements which it continues to generate. Eating balanced food is not sufficient to overcome the defilements. What is much more important is the mental reaction to our experience.

Let us now look at one of the oldest techniques extolled by all religions : morality. In a general sense, morality implies exercising control over our actions, refusing to give free license to our negativities and defilements. Many religions give primary importance to certain moral precepts : not killing, not-stealing, not-lying, avoiding sexual misconduct and refraining from intoxicants. What could be the purpose of following such precepts? Let us understand how the precepts of morality can help us to live a life of right actions. We can divide actions into three categories : actions at the physical level, actions at the vocal level and actions at the mental level. In our society, most people give more importance to physical actions than to vocal actions, and even less importance to actions at the mental level. But the mental action is in fact the most important, for it is this which gives birth to vocal and physical actions. For example, before we hit somebody, we speak biting words to him and before we speak those words, the will to injure arises in the mind. As it is volition that, gives birth to both vocal and physical actions, the action of the mind has the greatest importance.

'Mind leads all mental actions. Mind matters most. Everything is the product of mind. If one performs vocal or physical actions with the base of an impure mind, misery follows him like the wheel of the cart which follows the bullock yoked to it. If one performs vocal or physical actions with the base of pure mind, happiness follows him like the inseparable shadow." (Dhammapada, 1-2)

Two different persons can act in ways which appear to be the same, yet when their volitions are different, the resulting actions become completely different in moral significance and value. A thief plunges his knife into a man to steal his money and the person dies.

A doctor plunges his scalpel into somebody's stomach to cure an illness, but the operation fails and his patient dies. In both cases, outwardly the action seems the same and the result was the same, but the difference in the two volitions make them cases of totally different actions.

Morality and *right* concentration are the foundation-stones for right understanding, but even right understanding admits of levels. We can distinguish three levels of understanding: the *emotional or devotional* level, when we believe something out of faith in a teacher or in a set of scriptures. The *intellectual* level when we believe something because it appears rational and intelligible, and the *experiential* level, when we know something not only because somebody said so, not only because it is rational, but because we ourselves have experienced it. It is this third level of right understanding which alone can bring us to real happiness, and it is accordingly at this that we must aim in our spiritual practice.

The Missing Link

It was said before that right understanding, experiential right understanding, arises out of a concentrated mind, a mind which is calm and controlled. But how can we control our minds in order to get free from defilements? If we give free license to all our thoughts and impulses, our defilements only increase and multiply. If we try to suppress them in a blindly rigid manner, we become tense and anxious rather than calm and concentrated. The solution to true self-control is the Middle Path discovered and proclaimed by the Buddha, the Enlightened One. In following the middle path we neither give free license to our defilements, nor do we suppress them in a dogmatic, self-frustrating way. The path is to observe them objectively, with detachment, with equanimity, neither craving for what is pleasant nor arousing aversion towards what is unpleasant. In this kind of observation there is understanding of defilements without the generating of any further defilements.

Let us assume that anger has arisen in my mind. If I react immediately and ascribe this anger to an external cause—thinking "this person or this event is causing trouble for me" – the anger will only increase. Attributing the cause of a defilement to its outer stimulus leads me to identify with the defilement, thence to nourish it and give it greater strength. To overcome anger, we must learn to attend, not to the outer circumstances provoking the anger, but to the actual angry state of mind within ourselves. We must try to understand it from within rather than yield to it and connect it with outer causes.

Similarly, we must try to understand our entire psychophysical organism, the compound of body and mind which we call "myself". The Buddha has analyzed the individual into five groups of components, which He called the five aggregates. The *matter* constituting the body is one aggregate; the other four are mental. The first factor of the mind is *consciousness*. The senses cannot work unless they are connected to consciousness. When we are absorbed in a good book, our entire consciousness is riveted to our eyes; if somebody speaks, we do not even hear him because our entire consciousness is focused on what we are reading. This part of the mind is the one which cognizes, which knows the objective fields of the external and internal worlds. The second factor is perception which perceives objects and *recognizes* those objects that have previously been perceived. This faculty of recognition evaluates evry sensory stimulation. If a person speaks to someone, the auditor recognizes that the spoken words are either words of praise, words of abuse, or neutral. And from this comes the third factor, the feeling, or *sensation*. If he hears words of praise, he will have pleasant sensations, but if he hears words of abuse, unpleasant sensations will arise. The recognition arisen in the mind affects the body. For this is the Law of Nature, mind and matter are bound together. But our misery does not come from these three factors of the mind. The responsibility for our unhappiness lies in the fourth factor called the *sankharas,* the volitional formations. After sensations are experienced, volitions will emerge in the form of liking or disliking. the liking generally tends to turn into clinging and craving, the disliking into aversion, dissatisfaction and unhappiness. All the negativities of the mind come from this reactive part of the mind, from our reactions towards pleasant and unpleasant sensations caused by our evaluation of our sensory stimulation. This is the cause of suffering!

One who rolls in pleasant bodily sensations and has not understood wisely their true nature is not liberated from such sensations. This is the dormant conditioning of craving. One who reels in painful bodily sensations and has not understood wisely their true nature is not liberated from such sensations. This is the dormant conditioning of aversion. One who takes pleasure even in the tranquil bodily sensations which are neither pleasant nor painful, as taught by the infinitely Wise Buddha is also not liberated from misery. O meditators, when a meditator eradicates the dormant conditioning of craving for pleasant bodily sensations, the dormant conditioning of aversion for painful bodily sensations, the dormant conditioning of ignorance about neither pleasant nor painful bodily sensations, such meditator is called one who is totally free from dormant impurities, who has realized truth, who has cut off all the cravings, who has broken all bondages, who has fully realized the truth about the illusion of ego, who has come to the end of misery. (Samyutta Nikāya 36 Vedanāsamyuttam).

A Ten Day Retreat of Vipassanā Meditation

The Buddha taught us that we can free ourselves from defilements by means of insight, by understanding the nature of our own experience. One very powerful method of gaining this understanding is to contemplate the sensations connected with our defilements. We are to observe them calmly, with an equanimous mind, without reacting to them by way of craving and aversion. The objective is just to see things as they are, in their true nature, which the Buddha summed up by the three "marks" of impermanence, suffering, and non-self.

To grasp this technique of contemplation, to gain awareness of our sensations and develop equanimity towards their fluctuations it is immensely helpful to undertake an extended course of training in *Vipassanā* meditation. In the tradition of S.N. Goenka, the well-known Indian meditation teacher, such courses are generally given at the introductory level for a ten-day period. This period of retreat and intensive practice gives us the opportunity to focus all our energy and attention on the task of understanding the true nature of our being. When the period of training is over, one returns to the world and learns to apply the technique in one's day-to-day life.

In Pali language, *pāssana* means to look in the ordinary way, *Vipassanā* is to observe things as they really are, not only as they appear to be. It is to understand the impermanent nature of all things through our own experience. It is to experience this reality equanimously, without any reaction of craving or aversion. When we come to a ten day retreat of *Vipassanā* meditation, we come to practise three things; *sila, samādhi* and *pannā* (morality, right concentration and wisdom). The first step is to undertake five precepts: to abstain from killing, stealing, speaking lies, sexual misconduct and from taking intoxicants. We are also asked to observe complete silence–not to speak, read or write, but to direct all our attention inwards during the entire course.

The second step is the practice of concentration. At the beginning of the course, our mind is very agitated, so to calm it down, for the First three days we use our breath as the object of our meditation (anapanasati). This is not a breathing exercise; we do not try to control the breath, but just observe it as it is. The entire technique consists in moving from a subtle to a subtler field, from the conscious to the unconscious level of the mind. In our body, we know how the arms and the legs work. They work according to our volition, to our command. But many organs do not work this way, even if we want to stop our heart beathing, it will not. Unconsciously, our liver, our lungs, our heart, do not wait for our wishes to function. In addition to those big organs, all the atoms and the subatomic particles are constantly moving and we are not even aware of it. The breath can be a tool for us to introspect the unconscious field. It is the only function of the body that works both ways, intentionally and unintentionally. We can control our respiration to a certain extent, but if we leave it on its own, it will continue to function normally. We can use the breath as a bridge which can help us to cross from the conscious field to the unconscious one. So from 4.30 AM to 9.00 PM., we silently observe our breath with several breaks for breakfast, lunch, tea and rest. In this way, little by little, the mind settles down and becomes rightly concentrated.

When a negativity arises at the mental level, two things happen at the physical level; the breath deviates from its normal rhythm and certain biochemical changes occur in the body; these changes are experienced as sensations. So by observing the breath objectively, we not only gain control over the mind, concentration, but also obtain purification of the mind because the breath is related to our defilements. Thus by observing the breath, indirectly, we are observing the defilements. The first three days of the retreat are fully devoted to this *anapana* meditation because at the beginning the breath is easier to observe than the sensations, and at the same time we develop more concentration to enter a subtler field, the field of *Vipassana* meditation.

Having begun with gross reality, we move towards a subtler and subtler one, and on the fourth day, *Vipassana* is given and we plunge into the ocean of sensations, the gateway of wisdom. From the top of the head to the tips of the toes, we observe with increasing equanimity all the sensations we come across, in every part of the body, without craving for the pleasant ones, nor rejecting the unpleasant ones, just seeing things as they are.

"Here a meditator, when feeling a pleasant sensation understands properly, "I am feeling a pleasant sensation"; when feeling a painful sensation, he understands properly, "I am feeling a painful sensation"; when feeling a neutral sensation, he understands properly, "I am feeling a neutral sensation."
Now his awareness is firmly established in the present moment. This awareness develops to the extent that there is mere observation and mere understanding, nothing else, and he dwells in a state where he does not grasp

anything, and there is nothing for him to grasp in the
frame-work of the body. This is how a meditator dwells
observing bodily sensation in bodily sensation itself."
(Satipatthana-Vedananupassana)

When we start our observation of the sensations, it might be
difficult to develop the sensitivity of the mind, but with a continuous
practice, and with a strong equanimity, we calm our mind, and
thus increase our awareness which enables us to feel sensations—
which were always there–in the part that were blind before. Once
we feel sensations everywhere on the surface of the body, we direct
our awareness inside, and through the same process, start feeling
sensations deep inside. As we proceed in the ten day course, we
can go much deeper in our observation of the body. We will reach
a stage where we understand the composition of our body.

"There is in this body the element of earth, the element
of water, the element of fire, and the element of air."
(Satipatthana-Iriyapathabbam).

This does not mean that we will notice a particle of earth or
a drop of water in our body, rather we will come to know these
four elements by becoming aware of their qualities within ourselves.
The earth element has the quality of weight, from the lightest to the
heaviest; the water element has the quality of combining things
together; the fire element has the quality of temperature, from the
coldest to the warmest, and the air element has the quality of motion,
from the slowest to the fastest. All the material structures contain
these four elements and their qualities, and usually one element is
more or less predominant. Let us understand what determines the
predominance of a particular element. The food we take sways the
sensations of our body. The atmospheric conditions in which we
live is also bound to create some particular sensations. One who
lives in the midst of New York city would experience something
different than if he was living on top of a Himalaya mountain. The
food and the atomospheric condition are the two physical inputs.
There are also two mental inputs to which we shall attribute more
importance of the defilements we generate at this moment and the
defilements we had generated in the past. The defilements we

generate at this moment are bound to produce a sensation in our body. If we remain equanimous to this sensation, the defilement will automatically get eradicated. This process of eradication can be compared to the process of fasting. When somebody does not give food to the body, he does not die straight away. He can live for may be two or three months. What is happening? The body has to feed itself, so when no more food is given, it starts eating the old accumulated stock of food: all the fat of the body. When all the fat has been eaten and only the skin and the bones remain, the body has to die. Similarly, the mind has to be fed at each moment, either by craving or aversion. But when we are equanimous, no more defilements are generated, so the mind gets its food from the old accumulated stock of defilements. All the past anger, ill-will, animosity, lust, passion–all our past conditionings come to the surface of the mind and then produce more sensations on our body. Again, by remaining equanimous to these sensations, we can easily get rid of the past defilements to which the sensations are connected. This does not mean that when we will have perfect equanimity and when all our present and past conditionings, will be washed away, we will be lying down, doing nothing. No! Instead of living a life full of reactions begot by our past conditionings, our life will be filled with spontaneous, egoless actions, free from all taints and full of compassionate love.

Also, with this technique, while our awareness is spreading throughout the body, we realize the impermanence within ourselves. No sensation is eternal, not a single part of the body remains the same! At each moment, we experience the movement of the subatomic particles and we understand *experientially* how the mind works and how it keeps on reacting to different stimulations. Once we have experienced this impermanence, this non-solidity, we realize that there is no reason to cling to external things because the experience we have inside also reflects the outside reality. This understaning of the impermanence in all phenomena makes one realize that one has no control over anything, even on one's body. We continue to repeat "I", "me", "mine". If this body was really ours, why can't we stop it from decaying? This body is extraodinarily ephemeral, a mere mass of subatomic particles, arising and passing away at every moment! for conventional purposes, we have to say "I", "me", "mine", but we get trapped when these conventions take root in our mind and when we start developing attachment to them. Once one has experienced impermanence, this does not mean that one will go back in the society, stop working and tell everybody that they are a mere mass of subatomic particles. No! There are two levels of reality and we have to live with both of them in harmony. The other one is the ultimate level, the understanding of impermanence and attachment as the cause of suffering, ralization of which enables us to fulfill our duty without generating more defilement.

After ten days of diligent practice of awareness and equanimity, we learn a new meditation technique called *metta* meditation, the meditation of lovingkindness. Since the beginning of the retreat, we have been digging out our accumulated stock of negativities and on the tenth day, naturally we feel much more lightened and feel like sharing our peace and harmony with others. With the fruits we have gained, we generate thoughts of boundless love, compassion and peace towards all beings. These thoughts will not only affect our mind, but will affect our environment and eventually other minds as well. By practising *metta* meditation, we generate vibrations of pure love which will influence not only the surrounding atmosphere, but also the persons towards whom the *metta* is directed. After this meditation of lovingkindness, we break the Noble Silence and start chattering with other meditators. It is only the next day that we can return home. This small gap between *metta* and departure is essential to get used to the gross level of reality again before going back in the society.

How to Apply the Technique in our Daily Life

Now that we are back in our daily life, the real task begins. Because of this intensive meditation, we are rid of some very deep complexes which had been accumulated in the past. Having grasped this technique which brought so much peace, we feel like applying it in our day to day life to overcome agitation and to generate goodwill in all our actions. For this, we have to keep our volition as pure as possible by living a moral life and remaining aware and equanimous whenever a defilement arises in the mind.

Our old habit of mind was to constantly react whenever unwanted things happened and wanted things did not happen. In life, we would generate a lot of tensions within and start throwing our misery on others. But now that we have this technique of self observation, we know that whenever we are overpowered by a mental impurity, we lose the balance of the mind and become very unhappy. We now have two good friends inside to remind us whenever we become agitated. Indeed, the breath and the sensations will start to shout everytime a storm is about to erupt. The breath will lose its normality and some heat of tension will manifest itself in the body. The mere observation of these two will easily blow away the negativity. Of course, everyone does not become a saint after ten days of practice. But strengthening ourselves through meditation (which is not only in the sitting position) will bring us closer to the final goal of full liberation. For example, at the beginning, after an unpleasant incident, instead of boiling eight hours in anger, with the calm observation of sensations, we will boil only four hours, and as we proceed further it will decrease to one hour, then half hour,...until we reach a stage where nodefilements can overpower us anymore.

In this particular technique, one of the essential aspects is to maintain the continuity of practice. For this purpose, it is highly advisable to meditate in the sitting position two hours a day, morning and evening so that we continue to eradicate our old stock of impurities and turn the old habit of reaction into a new life of fresh, spontaneous actions.

The whole technique consists in cultivating three things : *sila, samadhi* and *panna* (morality, concentration or control over the mind, and wisdom). To make it clear, we can divide morality in three divisions : Right speech, Right action and Right livelihood. They consist of avoiding all actions (either vocal, physical, or mental) that may hurt another being. *Samadhi* is divided in three divisions; Right effort, Right awareness and Right concentration.

To be considered as "right", they must be directed towards the purification of the mind. *Panna* can also be divided in two parts : Right thought and Right understanding. Right thought comes naturally, as a consequence of the practice of morality and of control over the mind. It is thought free from impurities, free from anger, illwill, delusion,...Right understanding is what brings us to practice *Vipassana* meditation. It is by intellectual knowledge that we first get attracted to walk on the path of purification. But once we have started the journey, this intellectual knowledge yields its place to real understanding, the knowledge we gain by working on ourselves. Once we have developed some real understanding, it helps to strenghten our morality, which strengthen our concentration and reveals more wisdom to us...and the wheel keeps on turning, the wheel of liberation...

By investigating the truth about matter, we are bound to investigate the truth about the mind. By observing matter, which is one of the five aggregates, the five groups of components, we are bound to understand its relation to the four other aggregates. How does matter, through the six sense doors (sight, hearing, taste, touch, smell and thoughts) relate to consciousness, perception, recognition and reaction. This is not a mere theoretical understanding but what is called *patipatti,* the knowledge gained by practice, the understanding at the experiential level.

17
The Psychodynamics Of Vipassanā Meditation

Dr. C.V. Jogi

Being enlightened by Vipassana meditation learnt at Igatpuri I was tempted to delve deep into its dynamics.

This technique was developed by Siddhartha Gautama, the Buddha nearly 2,500 years ago. Today, thousands of people from different religious and cultural backgrounds are coming forward to learn this technique. Here is an attempt to show how it works.

Everyone in this world is in quest of peace and happiness and in this process one tries to find out the means for the same. In these days of modern civilization everyone is after pleasure which most of the time ends in pain. But one realizes this only when one gets pain which nobody wants. So long as one is in pleasure one never thinks of it. One feels happy, but begins to think only when one feels pain.

There are a number of people who indulge in pleasures of every sort and do not realise there is a limit to it. If in excess, it results in pain. This will depend upon the hereditary predisposition which is known as constitution. So long as there is adaptation to this pleasure - pain balance, nobody bothers about it but a day comes when this pleasure - pain balance tilts on the pain side and one tries to seek solace either by way of medicine, and if medicine fails to provide relief, one turns to meditation as a last resort.

---

* The Seminar on Vipassana Meditation, Vipassana Research Institute, Igatpuri (Maharashtra), December 1986.

All this is because of ignorance. It is rightly said that all illnesses start first in the mind and then go to the body. Many people do not understand this fundamental principle of aetiology of illness. But homeopathy is the first medical science which recognises this as the basic cause of illness. Everyone exists in three planes of one's life - the spiritual plane, the mental plane and the physical plane.

The Buddha teaches that everything existing in this world is 'anicca' (impermanent), so why bother about it? Therefore, the first advice is, not to worry even if any situation is not agreeable to you. This fundamental principle is repeated everyday in Vipassana meditation course. So everything is dynamic, nothing is static. Even pain which you may suffer from or pleasure which you may experience is not going to last long as it is 'anicca' (impermanent), so simply look at it or observe it with an undisturbed mind. This is the fundamental principle of Vipassana meditation.

When we utter the word 'dynamic', people do not understand it, as its meaning is very minute and subtle. Homeopathy defines disease as the dynamic derangement of the vital force. Since everyone has got energy and force which is continuously manifested throughout one's life in various ways, one is also affected by the various forces which are either intrinsic or extrinsic and because of such forces, balance of vital force is lost and man becomes ill.

Thus, human illness can be represented by the following diagram:

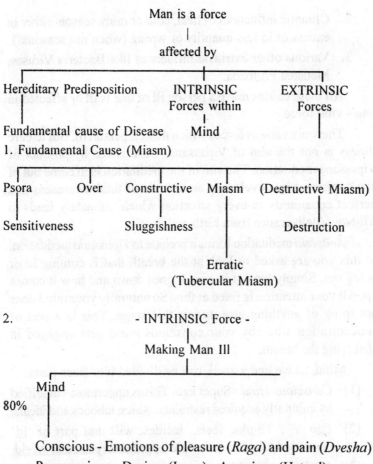

Man is a force

affected by

Hereditary Predisposition	INTRINSIC Forces within Mind	EXTRINSIC Forces
Fundamental cause of Disease		

1. Fundamental Cause (Miasm)

Psora   Over   Constructive   Miasm   (Destructive Miasm)

Sensitiveness   Sluggishness   Destruction

Erratic
(Tubercular Miasm)

2.   - INTRINSIC Force -

Making Man Ill

Mind
80%

Conscious - Emotions of pleasure (*Raga*) and pain (*Dvesha*)
Preconscious - Desires (Love) - Aversions (Hatred)
Subconscious - Attachment (Maya) - Ego (*Ahamkara*)
    All these emotions and various other emotions also are hidden at the subconscious level without our understanding them at the conscious level.

- EXTRINSIC Force -

1. Food - (*āhāra*) excess of it or deficiency of it.
   Eating of things which are not necessary for maintenance of life (*mithyā āhāra*).

2. Climatic influences of heat, cold or rainy season-either in excess or in less quantity or wrong (when not seasonal).

3. Various other extrinsic influences like Bacteria Viruses, Metazoa Protozoa.

All these causes make a person ill or one is ill or affected in one's vital force.

There are various forces which make a person ill. But to cure illness is not the aim of Vipassana. Cure is the by-product of Vipassana meditation. The aim of the meditation is to come out of one's miseries by developing an attitude of total awareness and perfect equanimity in every situation which ultimately leads to *Nibbāna* (deliverance from birth and death).

Ānāpāna meditation forms a prelude to *Vipassana* meditation. In this you are asked to look at the breath that is coming in or going out. Simply look at it, how it goes down and how it comes up. All your attention is fixed at this. So naturally your mind does not think of anything else during this stage. This is a sort of concentration whereby your conscious mind gets engaged in observing the breath.

Mind, as we understand, can be divided into three parts:

(1) *Conscious Mind :* Super ego. This is uppermost - modified by culturally acquired restraints, ethics, tabboos and ideals.

(2) *Ego 'I' :* Thinks, feels, decides, will that part of '<u>Id</u>' converted to reality principle by proximity to outer world.

(3) *Id :* Represented by unconscious.

I   Guarded by pursuit of pleasure and avoidance of pain.

II   Unorganised, timeless, out of contact with reality.

III   Logic has no place in *Id.*

IV   Lacking in morals of Ethical judgement and no sense of social values.

Id   -   unconscious

Ego -   preconscious and conscious

Super Ego -   conscious

So 'Ego' stands in between the 'conscious' and the 'unconscious'. During the process of *Ānāpāna* the conscious is held in abeyance because the thinking process is stopped. During the process of *Ānāpāna* because of full concentration on breath it naturally gets quieter and as the breathing process is quietened, the thoughts also begin to subside.

The mind has got great association with breath. If the mind is agitated, the breathing naturally becomes fast. This is an everyday observation. When breathing becomes subtle (rate is slowed down), the mind also stops thinking and *samādhi* (concentration) is achieved.

When conscious mind becomes quiet, the preconscious and unconscious mind come into play. They become dominant.

So, after satisfactory progress of *anāpāna,* or when concentration is achievd, you can understand the play of conscious as the various emotions of pursuit of pleasure and plain become dominant and come to the surface and when they are dominant they make some changes at the biochemical level of the body, and are represented by what is known as '*samvedana*' (sensation), or varous impulses, good or bad, which can be perceived during the process of Vipassana.

After sufficient practice of *anāpāna* you are asked to undertake the practice of Vipassana. This is an attempt to look at the unconscious.

When the conscious mind comes to zero activity through *Ānāpāna* meditation, the subconscious tries to come up and whatever emotions of pain and pleasure or attachment or ego are submerged at the conscius level are represented at the body level through various types of sensations. so you are to look at these sensations from head to feet as they manifest. Thus, indirectly through these sensations at the body level you can observe your subconscious mind.

This can be represented in a diagram as below: .

Body

Head; scalp

Face; eyes, nose, ears, tongue

Neck; front and back

Chest; front and back

Right Arm; front and back

Left Arm; front and back

Abdomen; front and back

Right Leg; front and back

Left Leg; front and back

Feeling	Thinking	Willing Mind	Action
Conscious - Super Ego			
Touch	Knowing	Under-stands whether good or bad	Reac-tion
Preconscious - Ego			
Subconscious - Id			

Right up to fingers.

Suppressed emotions come up and are represented at the body level through sensations because of biochemical reactions which are taking place at various levels - cellular, tissue, structural and organic.

During the process of Vipassana the subconscious is emptied and emotional conflicts because of the ego and super ego opposing each other are over as conscious is at zero activity. When these sensations come up you are simply to observe them without any expectations. You should not be sorrowful if sensations are painful and you should not, also, be joyful if emotions are pleasurable. You should also not make any attempt to bring up any particular type or types of sensations as it is not in your hand. *The only thing you have to do is to simply observe them without being led away.*

Mind and body are intimately connected with each other. Every emotion, for example, anger, hatred, indignation, attachment, love and craving is registered at the body level by way of certain minute changes at the biochemical level. These waves are electromagnetic in nature and we fail to observe them under normal circumstances as mind is engaged in outside activities.

Under the meditative process of *Anāpāna* and *Vipassana,* you may be able to observe these minute changes provided the activities of your mind are suspended and maintained at the 'O' Level.

During the process of *Anāpāna* which is not very difficult, your respiration slows down as the mind becomes concentrated. When the respiration is slow, the thought activity becomes slow. By the process of *Anāpāna* you can control your thought activity and thereby give rest to your conscious mind. When the conscious mind comes to 'zero' activity which can be achieved through this process, the preconscious and subconscous begin to come up and when they come up they begin to give vibrations at the skin level or even at the deeper body level. We know this through various types of sensations that manifest themselves. These sensations are simply to be observed.

Every sensation which you observe is nothing but a biochemical reaction or bio-electrical reaction. If these are observed with a balanced mind, the mind will become calmer and more peaceful.

Remember that all sensations, whether pleasurable or painful, are *'anicca'*, that is to say, lasting only for the time being.

This is what is known as *Vipassana* which one should practise with a balanced mind, with neither craving nor aversion. During such a process as one passes one's awareness through the body systematically, so many complexes and negativities get dissolved.

The preconscious and subconscious mind is a bundle of various types of emotions. The emotions which are not wanted are buried or repressed at the subconscious level.

Thus, during the process of Vipassana if you practise it correctly the subconscious mind is emptied and you become emotion free.

There are two principal types of emotions - love (*sukha*) and hatred (*dukkha*) and attached to these are 'I' (*aham*) or ego and another is *Maya* (attachment). Everyone possesses these in varying degrees. They are all responsible for misery and bondage of what is known as *Karma* (actions).

Vipassana makes you free from these bondages through a process of psycho analysis which occurs automatically, that is, without the help of any psychotherapist.

The aim of psychotherapist is to cure a person from illness while the aim of Vipassana is to give relief from sorrows permanently. Vipassana helps you to come out of the vicious circle of *Janma* (birth), *Jara* (old age) and *Maranam* (death) and rebirth. This is what is known as *Moksha* (*Nirvāṇa*).

With the regular practice of Vipassana many mental and physical ailments get eradicated. This is the by-product of Vipassana, not the aim. To practise Vipassana with proper understanding is known as *Paññā* (wisdom, insight).

18
Perfect Health Through Buddhist Mental Science*

Dr. B. Jayaram

1. The Universal Malady

Many today are willing to admit that the world is chaotic. There is conflict within and without, and it requires but little reflection to be convinced of the truth of universal suffering (dukkha). The following is from Winwood Reade's illuminating book, "Martyrdom of Man":

"... It is when we open the book of nature, it is when we read the story of evolution through millions of years, written in blood and tears, it is when we study the laws regulating life, the laws of productive of development, that we see plainly how illusive is the theory that God is love. In everything there is wicked profligate and abandoned waste. Of all animals that are born only a very small percentage survive. "Eat and be eaten is the rule in the ocean, the air, the forest. Murder is the law of growth...."

The doctrine of *dukkha* (suffering) is based on another universal fact which is *anicca* (impermanence, transitoriness). All is a flux, an everlasting becoming. Nothing is permanent. "Decay is inherent in all component things." This changeableness, this instability, cause dissatisfaction which leads to sorrow.

---

* Perfect Health Through Buddhist Mental Science by Dr. B. Jayaram, M.D., Maha Bodhi Society of India, Calcutta, 1955. (Abridged).

The third sign or condition of being is *anatta* (ego lessness). This is the doctrine of non-dependence, of the absence of an immortal soul. Nothing has a permanent inner unchanging core which exists eternally independent of other manifestations of life. Nothing is independent. From this it is but a short step to the world-wide belief in the unity of life, that everything we see is a part of a cosmic whole. It is a fact of nature and it peeps out in every page of the Dhamma. Hearken to the Buddha's pronouncement twenty five centuries ago:

> *"Whether Buddhas arise, O Brethren, or whether Buddhas do not arise, it remains a fact and the fixed and necessary constitution of being, that all its constituents are transitory (anicca), that all its constituents lack an enduring substance (anatta)".*

(Anguttara Nikāya)

Dr. Ranjan Roy in his essay on "Buddhism and Science" in the Maha Bodhi Journal says:

"....The three conservation laws: matter, mass, energy, held their sway throughout the second half of the nineteenth century. Nobody challenged them....These were the trump cards of those idealists who cherished the thought of something indestructible. Nineteenth century scientists professed them as the governing factors of creation. Nineteenth century philosophers dogmatised them as the fundamental nature of the universe....They conceived that the universe was filled with indestructible atoms....Just as the nineteenth century was drawing to a close, Sir J.J. Thompson and his followers began to hammer the atoms which readily began to detach small fragments. These fragments were electrons, all similar and charged with negative electricity. Atoms hailed by Maxwell as the imperishable foundation stones of the universe broke down. They got broken into tiny particles: protons and electrons charged with positive and negative electricity respectively....The concept of a fixed un-alterable mass abandoned science for good....In this century the univeral belief is that matter is being annihilated at every instant....

"The Buddhist Doctrine of *Anicca* (Transitoriness) is confirmed....All is perishable, all is immaterial....The course of the universe is a process of regrouping and dissolution, dissolution and regrouping...."

The trend of modern science is the denial of an ultimate reality, unity in diversity, any Ego. Modern science is the echoing of the Buddhistic doctrines of transitoriness (*anicca*) and of egolessness (*anatta*).

Major F. Yeats Brown, author of "Yoga Explained", etc., says:

"Students of history all over the world admit that the ethical and metaphysical principles of Buddhism remain unique and unparalleled in the cultural history of mankind. With the advent of modern science and its acknowledged conclusions Buddhism has once more become the creed that would lead to human salvation....

2. Diagnosis and Aetiology

All human beings are born with instinctive urges of various forms and degrees with a tendency to cling to extraneous matter. There is thus competition and conflict in the stress and strain, in the toil and trouble of existence (*dukkha*).

With corporeal growth there arises the feverishness of burning desires, thirst for material commodities, itch for sensuous gratification, and so forth traceable to infection with the germs of covetousness (*lobha*) until the mind advances to the stage of self-purification and inner "disinfection", which must come through individual personal exertion.

There is also psychic trauma and self-inflicted damage with pollution (in this life or in a previous one) of the blood stream leading to debility of mind and inefficiency of body generated through malevolence (*dosa*); from festering sores in the breast there originate ill-will, envy, jealousy, hatred, malice and so forth. These can be healed by easy and graduated doses of self analysis, self-culture.

Many there are bloated and puffed with self-conceit through ignorance of the oneness of all beings in the evolutionary process. Their vision is clouded by mists of prejudice. Countless numbers are groping in dark alleys of delusion resorting to "external applications" of charlatans in the expectation of securing relief.

Others are smothered by coils of superstition and irrational beliefs and fears through lack of knowledge (*moha*).

The perfect antidote is procurable through the Buddha's Noble Eightfold Path (or Prescription). Every student of Buddhism is cognizant of the three cardinal poisons that cause havoc to mankind: human selfishness (*lobha*), human ill-will (*dosa*) human ignorance (*moha*).

The development of health must be directed towards the elimination of ignorance as much as it is directed against disease, because ignorance (*moha*) is the fertile womb of ill-health, premature decay, pain and anguish. The strained heart, the thickened arteries, very high blood pressure, glandular troubles and a host of other dysfunctioning organs could all be steered clear off by a knowledge of moral hygience (*mettā, samādhi,* etc). The problem of individual well-being is no longer the selection of palliatives but the careful direction of organic growth through moral and spiritual education (*pannā*) into right habits of thinking and acting.

3. Aetiology or the Cause From Within

When man was lingering tardily in the nursery days of thought, when he was so bogged down in superstition, when he was as yet unable to get a firm grasp on the world of reality, he ascribed all his sufferings to the wrath of gods or spirits. So he resorted in the first instance to prayers, vows, genuflexions, prostrations, feasts, libations, sacrifices and so forth. But gradually mankind has been learning and is still learning in the long and painful self-adjustment to act as his own guide. In the later and modern stages he placed his trust on his systematized knowledge and his sense of goodness and is endeavouring with infinite toil to eliminate war, slavery, poverty, disease, and so on. The enlightened individual now depends on human aid not celestial.

The Buddha admonished :

"Be ye a light unto yourselves. Be ye a refuge unto yourselves. Betake yourselves to none other outward refuge. Hold fast to the truth as a lamp. Seek not for safety in anyone outside yourselves."

(Mahāparinibbāna Sutta)

"Though a man conquer in battle thousands and thousands of men, a yet greater conqueror still is he who has conquered himself, who has disciplined himself in his thoughts, words, and deeds."

(Dhammapada 103)

At every conceivable opportunity the Buddha strove to teach his followers to rely upon themselves in the development of their moral and intellectual powers and in attaining freedom from sorrow by their own personal endeavours, he himself merely teaching, guiding, directing, stimulating and encouraging them.

This doctrine of self-reliance arouses in the individual a sense of personal responsibility for social betterment. Help we can get from outside, but such help is often enfeebling in its effects. Help from within is invariably invigorating.

All true progress depends on oneself, all real advancement is determined by one's own exertions. The Blessed One has promulgated hundreds of ethical aphorisms like the following:

"By ourselves evil is done;
By ourselves we pain endure;
By ourselves we cease from wrong;
By ourselves we become pure."

(Dhammapada)

Though each one has to secure emancipation by oneself with a little human aid, each individual by serving others assists the welfare and betterment of mankind and at the same time marches on towards his own perfection.

The Enlightened One stressed with unwearing iteration the meaning and quintessence of religion as:

(1) *"Sabbapāpasana akaraṇaṁ*

(2) *Kusalassa upasampadā*

(3) *Sacitta pariyodapanam"*

This may be tersely expressed as (1) self-discipline (2) self sacrifice (3) self-development.

Dwight Goddard, author of "Buddhist Bible" says:

"....among the world's religious teachers, Gautama Buddha alone has the glory of having rightly judged the intrinsic greatness of man's capacity to work out his salvation without extraneous aid.

"If the worth of a truly great man consists in his raising the worth of all mankind who is better entitled to be called trutly great than the Blessed One, who instead of degrading man by placing another being over him, has exalted him to the highest pinnacle of wisdom and love...."

Brahmachari E. Taylor, author of "Buddhism and Modern Thought" says:

"....Man has been ruled by external authority long enough. If he is to be truly civilized he must learn to be ruled by his own principles.; Buddhism is the earliest ethical system where man is called upon to have himself governed by himself. Therefore, a progressive world needs Buddhism to teach it this supreme lesson...."

R.J. Jackson in his "Buddhism and Indian Thought" states:

"....The unique character of the Buddha's teaching is shown forth in the study of Indian Religious Thought. In the hymns of Rig-Veda (Hindu) we see man's thoughts turned outwards, away from himself, to the world of the gods. Buddhism directed man's search inwards to the potentiality hidden within himself. In the Veda we find prayer, praise, and worship. In the Buddhist books we find meditation (mind training) by our own strenuous efforts...."

In pre-Buddhist times, in the ancient Hindu (Vedic) system of salvation the means adopted were almost entirely through external means and outward formalities. The Blessed One gradually conveyed enlightenment by such teaching as:

"Not superstitious rites, not bathing in holy water, but loving kindness to all, self-control of lust, ill-will and such like unworthy thoughts, are the rites that ought everywhere to be performed."

(Dhammapada)

*"He who has realised the Truth, he who is perfect
in virtue and vision, he who fulfils his duties to
fellowmen gains freedom from woe."*

(Dhammapada)

When there was drought and the credulous folk were led by
Brahmin priests to offer animals sacrifices on the altar of gods and
goddesses, the Buddhist missionaries went about distributing food
to the needy out of their "begging" bowls and explaining and arguing
that if drought is caused by the anger of gods then plentiful rain or
a deluge indicated a superior state of morality.

4. Psychology and Physiology

There is no thought or inclination, feeling or emotion, that is
not accompanied by corresponding changes in the body or brain.
With every thought we add something to the cells of the body and
the neurones of the brain. If the thought is wholesome then the
something added will be health-giving. This is simply the outcome
of the law of cause and effect, which may also be defined as
mundane karma or this worldly karma.

Nothing in nature is static. Science teaches that everything
is waxing and waning, resolving and reshaping. We are every
moment changing for good or ill, for weal or woe. This is
unavoidable and depends entirely on our thoughts and actions. The
functions of various organs, the secretions of endocrine glands,
improve or deteriorate with our disposition, temperament, character.
This branch of modern mental science is termaed psychosomatics
or mind-body medicine.

The longer an emotion, such as resentment, hatred, and the
like, has dominated the thoughts the greater the indent made on the
physical constitution. These emotions are like corrosive poisons
imbibed in small doses: oppressive and destructive. In the same
way exalted sentiments such as universal beneficence are positively
reparative and salutary.

Sudden excitement provoked by violent anger, alarming news,
or petrifying fear, causes immediate mental and bodily dysfunction,
as for instance, rapid beating of the heart (palpitation). It may even

precipitate an abrupt end to life if the person has degenerate muscle fibres in the heart. These usually occur to people who have not practised self-discipline, self-analysis and so forth.

The mind is the most vital factor in life. It is a subtle power just as electricity is. It is the builder and organizer of human destiny. Twenty five centuries ago the Buddha reiterated in several *suttas*:

"All states arising have mind for their causing,

Mind for their master, of mind are the offspring.

He who with foul mind speaks or does action,–

Him pain pursues as the wheel dogs the ox-hoof.

All states arising have mind for their causing,

Mind for their master, of mind are the offspring.

He who with pure mind speaks or does action,–

Him bliss pursues, to him clings like his shadow.

By oneself alone is evil done, by oneself is one defiled.

By oneself is evil avoided, by oneself alone is one purified.

Purity and impurity depend on oneself.

No one can purify another."

(Dhammapada)

The message of the Buddha, the greatest of all teachers of mental culture, is that mind is absolutely supreme. We are what we are because of the character of our accumulated consciousness. We are the product of our mental processes and we can overcome any limitation imposed upon us by heredity or environment and can build a new environment by the directive power of the will.

The body is in fact the child of the mind. Whenever germs and microbes attacks the various organs of the body, they first gain a foothold because the ground is prepared for them by certain forms of vicious thoughts that have been harboured by the individual.

Hearken to the words of the Enlightened One:

"Not in the air, not in the caves of the mountains:

nay, nowhere in the wide world is there a spot where

*a man can escape the consequences of his evil
inclinations, evil thoughts, evil deeds."*

(Dhammapada)

5. Psychology and Health

How can man secure sound health through a knowledge of
the mental faculties? Let us first inquire what is sound health. Does
it mean muscular strength or never having had a day's illness. If
a person is endowed with overflowing vitality never having had
occasion to rub some soothing balm for a headache but is tense,
irritable, or cruel and inconsiderate to sub-ordinates, or lacked
initiative and cultural interests, can he be placed in the category of
one in prime health?

The Westerner concentrated all his attention on externals.
He placed enormous emphasis upon the claims of the physical
body. He sought emotional stimulus in speed, noise and glare. He
looked outside for interest and amusement. Gradually he began to
pay heed to inner forces, the manifestation of the mind; and there
has sprung up many new cults.

An analysis of some modern schools of thought and
philosophies would reveal in some disguised form the original
promulgations of the Buddha. The psychological and ethical
teachings in the *Abhidhamma, Dhammapada* and so forth are
given new names e.g. Parapsychology, Psychosomatics, New
Psychology, Ethical Culture, and so on.

In the Ethical Movement which originated in Europe in the
nineteenth century, it is held as a fundamental principle that whether
man is the creature of a day, or has an everlasting future, one's
duty remains "to know, to love all, and to do the right." The belief
in an immortal soul is banished. The explanation for what is the
real soul of man is that "it is surely not a disembodied ghost but
rather his complex moral character, the sum total of his thoughts,
words and actions."

The following from a rock inscription by the Buddhist Emperor
Asoka is illuminating:–

*"Wherein does religion consist? It consists in doing
as little harm as possible, in doing abundance of
good, in the practice of love and compassion with
no thought of personal reward but the good of
fellowmen."*

Professor C.G. Jung, author of "Psychology", etc., says:
"....In every religion, with the exception of Buddhism,
the powers of the subconscious mind were represented
by gods and demons....As a student of comparative
religion I believe that Buddhism was the most perfect
religion the world has ever seen. The philosophy of the
Buddha, the theory of evolution, and the law of karma
were far superior to any other creed. Christianity aimed
at satisfying the feeling, not the mind. Buddhism satisfied
both...."

6. Mind Power

There are some powerful forces in the universe which are
invisible and intangible and often silent. These may be productive
and beneficial or destructive and harmful. This is common
knowledge in regard to such mechanical forces as steam, electricity,
magnetism, and the like; but few have yet learned to apply this
knowledge to the domain of mind where thought forces are
continually being generated as magnetic thought waves for good
or ill.

Science has proved that every living organic cell is a generator
and receiver of electro magnetic vibrations, each kind of cell having
its own proper period of oscillation and being consequently in tune
for the reception of vibrations of a definite frequency and wave
length.

The significance of electro-magnetic vibrations in the form
of thought transference are known to many. Phenomena such as
telepathy, hypnotism, clairvoyance, have for ages past been regarded
as almost commonplace in the East whereas in the West they are
still new.

The Anguttara Nikāya (Book of Gradual Sayings) the fourth division oof *Sutta Pitaka* of the Buddha Dhamma deals with the psychology and ethics with its methods of self-training. The mind of man has different aspects. (1) There is the conscious mind arising from the frontal lobes of the brain which is capable of reason, judgment, investigation, deduction and so forth. (2) There is the sub-conscious mind originating in the back part of the brain in which reign the instinctive urges and animal appetites. It controls the nervous system and the functions of the various organs over which we have no control. (3) A portion of this area of the brain is also the store house of memory.

The conscious mind has the capacity to weigh, balance, scrutinize and judge. The subconscious mind obeys the most powerful suggestion given to it either by the individual himself (AUTO-SUGGESTION) such as wishing and hoping to get better day by day; or the thoughts and suggestions projected from one man's mind to another (HETERO-SUGGESTION) such as wishing another to improve in health.

The human mind is a subconscious magnet drawing to itself (in accordance with the law of attraction) the thoughts that we cherish. The individual who accommodates in his breast unworthy feelings of ill-will, hatred, malice and the like, repels others even without one's knowledge. Jealousy or contempt for other brings back an inevitable harvest in kind from fellow beings. Fear and worry about sickness if frequently indulged in attracts the very misfortunes which are dreaded. These debilitating negative emotions have the tendency to upset the even tenor of the functions of the glandular organs of the body.

7. Right Mental Diet

Man has amazing potentialities of mind (as mentioned under Psychology) but like treasure hidden in the mountain they are of little use to him until he has cleared away the dense matter that keeps them concealed from himself.

Before a person reaches invisible treasures by digging and excavating, he has to clear the surface and surroundings to shed ample light for the strenuous task ahead. Just as the rising sun dissolves the dark shadows so are all forms of evil put to flight by the searching rays of positive and constructive thoughts which shine forth from a heart fortified by confidence in oneself.

Our flesh and blood, our corporeal nature, though liable to droop and wither as age advances, our mental and moral faculties grow and thrive in proportion to the degree of moral hygiene inculcated from youthful days. Many of the most cheerful men and women in the world are those in their 60's, 70's or 80's who have learnt and practised ethical living.

The first lesson in ethical life is to deposit in one's bosom noble seeds of good-will to all. Hence the Buddha laid down instructions for making a beginning with Reflections on Four Sublime States (*Brahma Vihārās*).

The foremost act is the practise of unbounded love to all, first by one's thoughts then by deeds. Hearken to the Buddha-word:

*"As a mother , even at the risk of her own life
protects her son, her only son, so let everyone
cultivate towards the whole world, above, below,
around, a heart of love unstinted, unmixed, all-
encompassing."*

(Metta Sutta)

This meditation of love is to so adjust your heart that you long for the welfare of all beings including the happiness of your enemies. Not only *mettā* conduce to one's spiritual well-being and betterment but to physical improvement also. The influence of the mind over matter is a great reality. We have discussed elsewhere how thoughts of hatred are poisons not only metaphorically but actually as well. Similarly thoughts of compassion habitually entertained generate in the human system valuable chemical compounds which stimulate the cells to produce energy and vitality. *Mettā* thus has a tonic effect on the whole physical constitution.

The absence of bloodshed and carnage in the progress of Buddhism and its peaceful penetration in all countries to which it spread, can be attributed to the lofty doctrine of *Mettā* strengthened by the doctrine of rationality where the Blessed One proclaimed to his followers not to accept any teaching on blind faith (*Kālāma Sutta*). This has been referred to elsewhere.

The second meditation is that of pity (*Karunā*) in which you think of all beings in distress, vividly representing in your imagination, their afflictions and sorrows so as to arouse a deep commiseration for them in your heart.

> *"May suff'ring ones be sorrow free*
> *And the fear-struck courageous be*
> *May the distressed ones shed all grief*
> *And the sick find health's relief."*

(Dhammapada)

The third is sympathetic joy (*Muditā*) rejoicing in the happiness and prosperity of others, and freeing the mind from antipathy.

> *"He who rejoices in the well-being and happiness*
> *of others and harbours no ill-will or jealousy is a*
> *true nobleman."*

(*Udāna*)

The fourth meditation is on equanimity (Upekkhā). contemplation on how trivial are the pleasures of the senses; how fatal the consequences of evil actions and so forth; how you can rise above comforts or hardships, praise or blame.

> *"He is a happy man who is not moved, who is not*
> *elated or depressed by the eight attachments:*
> *Sorrow and joy, praise and blame, wealth and*
> *poverty, gain and loss."*

(*Sutta Nipāta*)

By engaging in these meditations let your heart grow and expand with an ever-widening love until freed from all selfish hankering, hatred, passion, it embraces the whole universe with thoughtful tenderness.

Allen Bennet in his "Lectures on Buddhism":

'Nowhere in the history of the world before Lord Buddha do we hear of any teacher of religion who was ever filled with such an all-absorbing sympathy and love for the suffering humanity. Few centuries after him we hear of wise men in Greece: Socrates, Plato, Aristotle, but they were only thinkers and seekers after truth without any inspiring love for the suffering multitude....''

8. Health Through Our Thoughts

There lives an echo, a reverberation in our thoughts and emotions that expands in volume for good or ill. There is a fate at our heels, a fate of our own making that pursues us at all times, absorbing our thoughts and growing in multiple ratios on such echoes. This is a magnetic force that is ever with us by day and by night to lead us aright or fling us astray, to protect and preserve us or weaken and endanger us according to our desires.

The man whose heart is constantly bathed in silvery sprays of the sparkling fountain of *mettā* will be brimful of glowing vitality; spiritual flowers of gladness will bloom within his breast diffusing its sweet ambrosial fragrance far and wide. It is an etherial quality that will enliven and cheer him in the darkest moments of life, even in the midst of a devastating plague.

Let us recollect the oft quoted saying of the Blessed One:

"All that we are is the result of what we have thought, it is founded on our thoughts, it is made up of our thoughts."

(Dhammapada)

9. Elimination Of Poisons From Heart

The human mind may be compared to a garden. It is not sufficient to uproot weeds for they will shoot up again and again unless flower plants or fruit trees or grains are cultivated. A vaccum is not tolerated by nature.

The noteworthy method of dealing with evil propensities of the mind, of neutralizing acids and poisons in the heart, is to apply the antidote by fostering wholesome sentiments. Overcome evil not by merely keeping away from evil but by performing praiseworthy actions at the same time.

One of the often-repeated mandates of the Buddha is as follows:

> "Be hasty in performing good deeds while warding off your mind from evil. If one is slow in doing good, one's mind delights in evil."

(Anguttara Nikaya)

Dr. A.B. Holmes, author of "Buddhism and Psychology" says:

> "The great trouble with humanity is its absorption in the lower self and its manifestations, and this is where Buddhism shows us a better way....
>
> ....The magnetic power of Buddhism lies in its insistence upon the latent goodness in every human being. It carries a message of hope to even the most abandoned criminal whose divine nature is thickly overlaid with ignorance, but no ignorance is so dense that it cannot be pierced by the words of a great spiritual teacher.
>
> ....Buddhism is the religion of Hope, of Enlightenment, of Serenity, because it shows man that the path of knowledge is open to all...."

10. Health Through Character

Character is *karma* (action) crystallized. Let us recall the old adage:

Sow a thought and reap an act,

Sow an act and reap a habit.

Sow a habit and reap a character,

Sow a character and reap a destiny.

One's character is influenced by the example of a parent, a guardian or a close associate. Life begets life in the moral as well as the biological sphere. Moral growth is a process of adaptation and assimilation but no guide should be blindly obeyed or his behaviour unquestioningly assimilated. We should remember the Buddha's injunction in *Kalama Sutta* not to accept anything with uncritical faith or slavish attachment.

Character is developed when life is lived under the stress of skilful activity. Just as the diamond which has been subjected to severe pressure, so life which is lived under intense moral exertion and firm resolution for varying periods of time produces the jewel character which can shed a luminous glow in the darkest hour of trial and tribulation and which is capable of carving out a way to safety out of danger, out of misery, out of disease.

11. Self-Culture For Joyous Health

Buddhism teaches the method of extirpating evil through self-reliance, self-analysis, self-culture, self-development and so forth. It differs from other religions like Christianity which set faith and ritual above purity of morals. Buddhism gives you certain facts, a clear recognition of which will disentangle you from the tribulations of life. It emphasizes the certainty of the law of cause and effect in the moral plans not less than in the physical, that every thought, word and deed take their inevitable consequences, good or evil, according to their character.

Self-culture has three phases: (1) Discipline (2) Dedication (3) Development.

"I adjure you, O disciples, for your own sakes be diligent. Devote yourselves to the purification of your own minds. Be earnest, be persevering, be attentive to the welfare of hummanity."

(Mahāparinibbāna Sutta)

"Whose lives his life looking not to pleasure but with thoughts well controlled; regulated in his eating, virtuous, diligent in doing good–death (premature) can no more overthrow him than the storm the rocky mountain."

(Dhammapada)

Self-Discipline

This has three aspects:

(A) Discipline of Thought
(B) Discipline of Speech
(C) Discipline of Bodily Actions.

Discipline of Thought

In the Dhamma within the category of unworthy or ugly thoughts are included thoughts of hate, envy, revenge and the like; deceitful thoughts, conceited fearful thoughts. These are described as beastly thoughts in that they issue from the heart of lower animals.

To be substituted in their place are the following: disinterestedness, earnestness, benevolence, simplicity, modesty, patience and so forth.

"Let us guard the doors of the senses. Let us be restrained in our eating. Let us vow ourselves to earnestness and arm ourselves to earnestness and arm ourselves with an intelligence unclouded and be free from miseries."

(Majjhima Nikāya)

Be patient with all. Anger leads one to a pathless jungle. While it irritates and annoys others it also hurts oneself, weakens the physical frame and distrubs the mind. A harsh word, like an arrow discharged from a bow, can never be taken back even if you should offer a thousand apologies for it.

"One should give up anger, one should renounce pride, one should overcome all fetters. Ills never befall him who clings not to mind and body and is passionless."

(Dhammapada)

Earnestness (*Viriya*) is one of the most dynamic of virtues. It consists in choosing self-development instead of pleasure as the principal aim in life. Those who are lured by pleasure find their path ending in ennui, disease, stunted personality. Earnest man's chief attribute is simplicity. Simplicity is for the spirit what athletics are for the body.

Listen to the words of the Blessed One:

"Riches, beauty, perfumes and jewels are no such adornments as is right behaviour. True beauty, perfumes and jewels are no such adornments as is right behaviour. True beauty and true happiness are only to be found where right feelings have their home in the heart."

(Dhammapada)

The virtue of modesty is indispensable to personal happiness and an efficient social life. One should learn to take no heed of the opinions of others if one is convinced of the right path. A vain man or woman is often the slave of others. He is rude in manners and lacks courtesy in speech. Even if a person is superior to others in some respects one should ever be on guard against the sin of pride.

"Above all things banish the thought of "self". Keep yourself free from all evil to become noble."

(Udāna)

Discipline of Speech

The commonest evils issue from the tongue. The vast majority are little concerned in the misusage of speech such as harsh words, tale-bearing, lying, gossip and so on. Here are some utterances of the Tathāgata :–

"Courtesy is the most precious of jewels. Beauty without courtesy is like a garden without flowers."

(Buddhacarita)

"Forbearance and friendly speech; communion with the earnest and striving; discourse concerning the doctrine in fitting season–this is a great blessing."

(Mahāmangala Sutta)

Discipline of Bodily Actions

Those who commit evils of body reap a pernicious harvest. Killing, stealing, misconduct, drunkenness are injurious to oneself and damaging to others. Wrong actions generate in oneself callousness, hard-heartedness, recklessness that will ultimately ruin one's health and become destructive to social life.

If a man sacrifies moral development for fleeting joys he will never feel the enduring felicity and exaltation that are the fruits of self-mastery.

He who chooses sensual delights spends too much energy, resources and time in trying to live for the moment but ending in lethargy, fatigue and boredom. He is only catching the foam and froth of life because he is too indifferent to dive deep in search of priceless pearls and hidden treasures.

Self-Sacrifice

The doctrine of renunciation (*Nekkhamma*) (non-attachment) is a potent means of achieving inward peace and lasting bliss. It is the central sun around which all the other virtues revolve like planets. It stimulates the exertion of generosity and unselfish liberality. It entails the practice of self-control. It impels the cultivation of knowledge for insensitive stupidity is a main root of all the other vices. It necessitates courageous action. It is an incentive to the observance of patience, honesty, truthfulness, compassion, tranquility. It prompts altruistic social service for the promotion of human well being.

Here are some precepts from the Dhamma:

"Unselfish liberality, goodwill, courtesy–these are to the world what the linch-pin is to the chariot."

(Singālovāda Sutta)

"Even if the body is clothed in the layman's dress, yet may the mind mount to the highest things. The man of the world and the hermit differ not from one another if both alike have conquered selfishness.

*So long as the heart is bound to earthly bonds, all
outward tokens of the ascetic are useless."*

(Dhammapada)

The acquisitive instinct which is praiseworthy within
reasonable limits is being allowed to assume undue dimensions.
Material things tend to crush and strangle human personality and
work havoc with all progressive movements. If all the ardent,
intelligent well educated young men and women are avaricious
who will initiate uplift movements and organizations? It is only the
truly noble hearted men and women, who are free from avarice,
that can nurse new ideas and help forward humanity.

Self-Development

Self-development has three branches (1) Moral, (b)
Intellectual, (c) Physical. Moral aspect has already been dealt with.

Intellectual Development

Knowledge is like a deep well, fed by perennial springs, and
the mind of man is like a bucket that is dropped into it. He will get
as much as he can assimilate.

Knowledge and mental self-culture will confer incalculable
blessings to man. One third of the ills of man are due to human
ignorance, delusions and superstitious beliefts; the rest of the ills,
according to the Dhamma, are traceable to human selfishness and
human malevolence.

The Buddha with tireless emphasis proclaimed the necessity
to acquire knowledge, to study, and to meditate but not to accept
any doctrine or teaching on blind faith. (*Kālāma Sutta*).

Everyone should study ancient classics, various philosophies,
and progressive movements of East and West. "Histories make
men wise" said Bacon. History with Archaeology is certainly one
of the many sources of intellectual enjoyment. It is a refreshing
mental tonic. Psychology and physiology will teach people many
valuable lessons.

"There is no deliverance for those who are blinded by ignorance."

(Dhammapada)

"Long is the night to the watcher. Long is the way to him who is weary. Long is the world-wandering to beings grouping in ignorance and knowing not the truth."

(Dhammapada)

Physical Development

One of the mot fundamental requirements for physical and mental improvement is deep breathing exercises. This is a primary requisite in meditation. In the Buddhist Scriptures there is also mentioned the need for walking several miles a day, frequent bathing, light clothing, fresh air and so forth.

As regards food the following are prescribed as health promoting in *Lankāvatāra Sutra:* "Rice, wheat, barley; greens that are edible; many varieties of beans (especially the kidney-shaped bean), peas, gram, lentils (dal); nuts; oil from edible nuts; clarified butter; honey, molasses, coarse sugar, etc.–"

There is no mention of meat, eggs, etc. Many advanced thinkers and medical savants are of opinion that vigorous health is attainable without animal food provided that protein food such as peas, beans, gram, lentils (dal) are included in the daily menu.

The Buddha has not completely forbidden flesh food to his followers as there are individuals, who though capable of leading an ethical life and practising lofty virtues, may require meat for sustaining health.

"Those in this world who are unrestrained in their behaviour towards others, who are wicked, cruel harsh–of these, and not of the mere eating of flesh food, we may utter the word 'unclean'."

(Āmagandha Sutta)

12. Spiritual Sanitation

Meditation is the main entrance to the palace of peace, contentment, health and perfection. The cultivation of moral and mental aspects is a medicine that is more than a bracing tonic.

The various methods of inward purification will gradually transform a sickly constitution into one of unbounded vitality. They will confer elasticity and tone to the blood vessels, cutting short any tendency to high blood pressure, coronary thrombosis and other unspeakable agonies.

Physical conditions are largely determined by mental states. The body is what a man makes by the form of his thoughts. Medical men are ceasing to believe that a man is despondent or irritable because he has a weak digestion or is dyspeptic and are realizing that he is dyspeptic because he is irritable and despairing.

If you are given to worry and restlessness or frequently fly to a towering rage, or inordinately seek to quench burning desires, then you have not yet begun to strike the rich vein in the gold mine within you.

As already explained unwholesome, unworthy, ugly thoughts are termed negative or destructive emotions. Such states of thought are far more perilous than infected houses or polluted water.

Here is the Buddha's warning:

"Think not lightly of evil, saying: It will not come nigh me. Drop by drop the pitcher is filled. So the fool becomes saturated by evil, little by little he gathers it. The wise man gathers worthy thoughts and deeds, bit by bit he builds his pile of happiness."

(Dhammapada)

An individual lacking in earnestness and aspires not to attain high mental and moral stature is akin to a dwarf. He does not realize what surging tides of enduring joys he is missing, just as a man born blind cannot measure his loss. He who is devoid of spiritual ambition permits his valuable mental mechanism to deteriorate. If you allow rust to corrode a machine it will come to grief. By timely cleansing and lubrication you will secure long and efficient service.

In the Dhamma we find:

*"By prompt removal of thought of lust, anger, malice
and of a sinful and evil disposition, a man would
not be nursing the impurities, and he has no dread
of them nor of the untold suffering that comes in
their wake."*

(Majjhima Nikāya)

Methods of Inward Health

Ānāpāna Sati

The foremost item is deep breathing exercises a few times at the commencement. Deep respiration ensures a healthy nervous system. Ample air is an indispensable requisite for all the processes of life. Fill the lungs with air, and though at first it does not bring pleasure, soon you will feel better and stronger.

Cattāro-Brahmavihāra

Meditate on the Four Sublime States: Mettā, Karunā, Muditā, Upekkha. These have been described under the heading elsewhere RIGHT MENTAL DIET.

Samsāracakka Bhāvanā

The realization that everything in nature is characterized by transitoriness (*anicca*), unsatisfactoriness (*dukkha*), egolessness (*anatta*) paves the way to mental peace and serenity. And this meditation helps the control of emotions and passions, keeps away worries, troubles, temptations and other disturbing factors out of the mind. Diseases such as high blood pressure, nervous disorders are allayed or cured.

Sīla Sikkhā Bhāvanā

In this meditation one should ponder on the day's happenings – and this may be done just before falling asleep and while taking deep respirations. Have you committed by thought, word or act anything prompted by selfish handkering, lust, ill-will, envy, malice and so forth? Now promise to yourself you will do better next day by thinking and speaking and acting altruistically, benevolently and reasonably.

One may also think retrospectively over the day that is past. Has anyone done something to vex you or worry or even insult you? Place him before you in your mental vision and send him thoughts of forgiveness and inwardly whisper: "Peace, goodwill and happiness to you" and repeat this several times however disagreeable it may be at the time, you will have reaped a rich harvest of inward tranquility cleaner blood stream from absence of hatred.

13. Purgation of Hindrances

In the pursuit of cnquest over evils which is a positive quest there are obstacles to be overcome. In the elimination and cure of disease the barriers in the path are very much the same.

In the *Satipatthāna Sutta,* the Tathāgata has enunciated ten impediments to salvation of which the following only are touched upon here.

(1) Sensual disposition (*Kāmacchanda*)

(2) Malevolence (*Vyāpāda*)

(3) Indolenee (*Thīnamiddha*)

(4) Ignorance (*Avijjā*)

(5) Restlessness, worry (*Kukkucca*)

Sensual Disposition

A man's inherent vitality derived from parents or grand-parents is capable of sustaining him in fair condition despite excessive indulgence. For several months or years many individuals may with impunity disregard all the rules and laws of health but the inevitable crash is bound to come in due course.

Gluttony is the source of most of the infirmities past middle age. It unduly stimulates the sex organs. It is the spring and fountain from which flow ninety per cent of the diseases of the heart and blood vessels, liver and kidney and so forth. As a lamp is choked by superabundance of oil, a fire extinguished by excess of fuel, so is natural health undermined by excessive devotion to Baccus or Venus.

In order to surmount sensual propensities, it is vitally important to practise right mindfulness. One must thoroughly comprehend the existence of such dispositions when they arise. For instance when a voluptuous inclination is present he must realise that such an inclination is existing in himself and must then switch his mind on lofty thoughts or even a mechanical hobby. By sustained endeavour his mind will gradually come to a state of happier disposition of mind and body.

Meditation on the doctrines of transience (*anicca*), egolessness (*anatta*) is also helpful to combat unworthy inclinations. Whenever the sensual disposition is inordinate and is a burning desire towards some attractive person one is advised to dwell on the inevitable course of life on earth, as a sick and emaciated one, a toothless, grey-haired aged one, a corpse swollen and putrefying with maggots swarming, and so on.

"Unceasingly should the wise purge their hearts of dross as the smith refines the silver."

(Dhammapada)

Malevolence

In order to keep the blood stream in an optimum state of richness the constant thoughts should be those of good-will, sympathy, fellow-feeling.

Some varieties of heart trouble, rheumatic disorders, skin diseases are traceable to chronic resentment, hatred, jealousy, and so on. Such destructive feelings poison the cockles of the heart. They foster the development of latent disease tendencies and invite disease microbes.

When an unworthy motive has invaded the mind one must, while warding off such a disposition, substitute in its place good-will, appreciation and ensure furtherance whenever possible by good performances.

One should reason out the fact that wherever an estimable and praiseworthy quality is found it is something creditable to humanity. Whenever some extra-ordinary ability or virtue is found in another one must approve it and rejoice over it as a socially beneficent force that is bound to widen the circle of good in which he lives.

In the same way avoiding pride cultivate modesty, eradicate self-centred cravings and advance towards unselfishness and so on.

> *"Those in this world who neglect their duties to fellowmen, who do not approve the good and encourage the good, who are slanderers—of these may we utter the word unclean."*
>
> (Āmagandha Sutta)

Indolence

He who conquers indolence conquers all other inborn defects and shortcomings. Without activity all good principles stagnate and decay. Lack of exertion is like rust to the various organs of the body. Occupation is necessary for the mind as well as the body in order to maintain and advance in sturdy stamina. Sloth wastes the sluggish body as water turns impure unless it moves.

Mental toil offers the fairest fruits and richest rewards. Activity in the ethical plane, the exercise of moral virtues is a never-failing fountain spring of felicity in course of time. To heal the wounds caused by burning desires, unregulated passions and blind instincts is a matter of positive urgency.

> *"Better it is to live for one day with energy strongly stirred up than to live for a hundred years sluggish in energy."*
>
> (Dhammapada)

Ignorance

This is a formidable obstacle on the way to joyous health. In the domain of medicine we know how the individual uninformed regarding the elementary laws of health is a prey to ninety per cent of the ills of the flesh.

Knowledge and compassion are the two wings by which man can soar to regions of bliss supernal, by which lasting peace and happiness on earth can prevail.

"The three causes of sorrow and suffering are ignorance, malevolence and covetousness."

(Dhammacakkapavattana Sutta)

"By effort wisdom is achieved
By heedlessness wisdom is lost.
Consider well the double path of rise and fall and choose the path following which wisdom grows and increases."

(Dhammapada)

Worry

"Worry dries up the blood sooner than age." Fears, worries and anxieties in moderation are natural instincts of self-preservation. But constant fear and prolonged worry are unfailing enemies to the human organism. They derange the normal bodily functions (described elsewhere).

Fear either as a principle or a motive is the beginning of manifold evils. The notion of incurring the displeasure of a Creator are instilled into the minds of the followers of Semitic faiths. To the Buddhist nothing is to be feared but a stigma on character which is in his power to counterbalance and put right. And so it does not weigh in his bosom as a disturbing element.

Fears for the Future

In consequence of unfavourable predictions by astrologers in the event of ill-health there may be harmful reactions.

A sufferer who believes in fate would think: "This was preordained, this was allotted to me by God; so I must submit."

If he believes in karma he will reason as follows: "This is the result of my own activities in a previous life or in this life itself. I must try to rectify the balance of justice by strenuous exertion in doing good, but for the present I must meditate on Four Sublime States etc."

Through karma the individual grows and changes for better or worse from moment to moment, so that if we resort to meditation (mentioned elsewhere) there is good karma accumulating here and now. This is present karma or this worldly karma.

The Buddha has condemned astrology in no uncertain terms. In the *Brahmajāla Sutta* (Dīgha Nikāya I, 9-10)

"Whereas some recluses and others earn their living by wrong means of livlihood, by low arts such as these, palmistry, prophesying long life, prosperity, etc. (or the reverse) from marks on a person's hand, feet, etc.; divining by means of omens and signs; auguries drawn from celestial portents; prognostications by interpreting dreams; foretelling the future, Gotama keeps aloof from such low arts."

In the *Mangala Jātaka* (No. 87) we read the following:

"Whoso renounces omens, dreams and signs,
That man from superstition's errors freed,
Shall triumph over the paired depravities
And o'er attachments to the end of time."

The Buddha has also explained to his disciples (Majjhima Nikāya VII):

"To the energetic all days are auspicious
To the pure all days are holy days
They that are pure of thought and word and deed
They always have their work fulfilled."

There is no such theory as inevitable fate or irrevocable destiny in Buddhism. We can often observe how certain faults we committed yesterday are alone responsible for the unhappiness or ill-health we experience today. Hearken to the Buddha word:

"We are heirs to our deeds; our deeds are our heritage; our deeds are our inheritance."

(Anguttara Nikāya)

It should be clearly grasped that no destiny is definite. A destiny is only relatively durable; therefore Buddhism teaches no eternal hell or immortal heaven. It teaches cause and effect and incessant change (*anicca*). Thus a man may learn to master his nature and free his mind.

14. Noble Eightfold Prescription

(1) Right Views (*SammāDitthi*)

(2) Right Aspiration (*SammāSankappa*)

(3) Right Speech (*Sammā-Vāca*)

(4) Right Conduct (*Sammā-Kammanta*)

(5) Right Living (*Sammā-Ājīva*)

(6) Right Effort (*Sammā-Vāyāma*)

(7) Right Mindfulness (*Sammā-Sati*)

(8) Right Concentration (*Sammā-Samādhi*)

Right Views, Beliefs

This is the most essential step for progress on the path to deliverance. By realization of the ever present suffering (*dukkha*) of the impermanent nature of all component things (*anicca*) one gets an understanding of the egolessness of all beings (*anatta*). Then one learns to abandon selfish craving and grasping, provided he devotes a few minutes daily to contemplation on the subject.

The Buddha beckoned his followers to face facts and to refrain from accepting anything on blind faith.

In the *Kālāma Sutta*, the Blessed One insisted:

"Believe nought on mere heresay
Be not imposed by ancient sway
No truth because by custom taught
Nor in net of tradition caught

Accept not on witness of sage
Or written on hoary page
Though taught by a teacher sublime
Not ev'n sacred books are divine
But trust what accords with reason
And after test and reflection
That which leads to moral welfare
Stick by and to follow prepare."

To learn to come to grips with sorrow and suffering, to strip it of all the veils that hide its causes from us, this is what Buddhism requires of us. It is opposed to grovellings, to prayers and genuflexions, to cowardly concessions, to the giving up of the use of our thinking principle. It demands that our energy remain unimpaired, our minds lucid, our wills inflexible while we progress on the Path, ever in search of greater knowledge, better light, more right views.

Right Aspiration

The doctrine of the Buddha does not encourage the killing of all desire. He gave the answer in the *Majjhima Nikāya* and *Sutta Nipāta*.

Desires are of two kinds, the noble and the ignoble. Noble desire prompts man to works of compassion, to do good deeds and give the merits to others. Meritorious desire prompted the great Buddhist King Asoka to send missionaries to civilized countries of his time.

It is ignoble desire that makes men adopt the policy of Machiavelli, to distribute intoxicating liquor, opium and so on. Low desires are prompted by self-centred longings (*tanhā*) born of ignorance.

Right Speech

The disciple learns to abstain from uttering falsehood, from indulging in tale-bearing and from repeating anything which he has heard that might cause enmity and discord, feuds and factions, quarrels and disputes among fellow beings. He takes pleasure in establishing harmony by his words that are always gentle, kind, and agreeable. Though careless speech is to be avoided one should not be afraid to speak out the truth where duty demands, even if it may cause some displeasure.

"Oh, one should speak the word
That seareth not himself,
nor yet another harms:
That is the goodly word;
Should speak the kindly word,
Words that make others glad,
Words that bear ill to none,
Of others kindly speak.
Truth is the deathless word,
'Tis ancient Dhamma this."

(Sutta Nipāta –
Woven Cadences 451–453)

Right Conduct or Action

Right conduct means abstaining from intentional killing, falsehood, dishonest taking, adultery, intoxicating drinks and drugs.

The preliminary rules of morality the Five Precepts (*Panca Sila*) propounded by the Enlightened One 25 centuries ago is now the common ethical code of the civilized world. This code, apparently negative, is in reality the store house of positive virtue because the expulsion of vice prepares the ground for the development of good character, which goes on increasing in the path of self-culture.

"Whoso hurts and harms living beings, is destitute
of sympathy for any living thing, let him be known
as an outcast."

(Vasala Sutta)

"The real treasure is that laid up through charity
and pity, temperance and self-control. The treasure
thus hidden is secure and passes not away. Though

he leaves the fleeting riches of the world, this a man
carries with him—a treasure that no wrong of others
and no thief can steal away."

(Nidhikaṅḍa Sutta)

Right Living

The disciple refrains from wrong way of living. To practise deceit in a transaction would be incorrect living; so is usury, sooth-saying, fortune telling; so is manufacture of arms or intoxicating liquors.

Here are some stanzas from the Scriptures:

"Let no one neglect his own duty for that of another
however great it may be. When he has clearly
perceived his own duty let him apply himself
diligently thereto."

(Dhammapada)

"Whoso strives only for his own happiness and in
so doing deprives others of their happiness he shall
find no real happiness here or hereafter."

(Dhammapada)

"So lives the disciple as a reconciler of those that
are divided, as one who binds still more closely those
that are friends; as an establisher of peace; a maker
of peace; ever a speaker of peaceful words."

(Tevijja Sutta)

Right Effort

There are four efforts which the follower of the Noble Path strives to develop. (1) The first is the effort to discard evil. Thus when he sees a form with the eye or hears a sound with the ear, he strives not to be drawn by it and watchfully restrains his sense. (2) The next is the effort to prevent the arising of new evil. He does not entertain thoughts of sensual lust, greed and the like. (3) The effort to develop fresh meritorious conditions. (4) The endeavour to maintain existing wholesome conditions and develop them to full maturity.

This step in self-discipline will help a man to keep out of gluttony, intemperance, sexual excesses. Thus diseases of the heart, kidney, liver, etc. are easily avoided or kept under control.

Never to be disheartened but ever to strive and struggle is the counsel of the Blessed One:

"May rather skin, sinews and bones wither away, may the flesh and blood of my body dry up, I shall not give up my efforts so long as I have not attained whatever is atainable by manly perseverence, human energy, personal endeavour."

(Dhammapada)

"Overcome that desire to which both gods and men are so completely subject. Let not the right moment escape thee. Those who have allowed the fitting time to pass away unused will have good cause to lament when they find themselves upon the downward path."

(Uṭṭhāna Sutta)

"The man enmeshed in delusion will never be purified through the mere study of holy books, or sacrifices to gods, or through fasts, or sleeping on the ground or the repetition of prayers. Neither gifts to priests, nor the performance of rites and ceremonies can work purification in him who is filled with craving. It is not through the partaking of meat or fish that a man becomes impure but through drunkenness, deceit, envy, self-exaltation, disparagement of others and evil intentions–through these things man becomes impure."

(Dhammapada)

Right Attentiveness

In the domain of physical health this step will definitely cure insomnia and mental worry, and will ensure freedom from high blood pressure.

Details of this step in mental and moral culture are found in *Satipaṭṭhāna Sutta* of the Dhamma.

Practise the following for a few minutes daily (1) *Kāyānu Passanā* (mindfulness of body). The disciple is first asked to contemplate the body in its most important functions, namely the operation of breathing–In Exhaling a deep breath, then a short breath, etc. No other thought should be permitted to invade the mind. What is aimed at is tranquilized breathing coupled with a complete awareness of the breathing process that is going on.

The second type of Right Attentiveness (*Vedanānupassanā*) as regards sensation or feeling. These must be considered objectively. When he experiences a pleasurable sensation he is aware of it as such, a painful one as such. It is not "I am feeling" but "There is a feeling". The habit of looking objectively at our feelings and impressions have a salutary effect in aiding us to maintain an even tenor of life, free from flurry, worry or excitement.

Right Concentration

This step is for perfect moral and spiritual status that leads to perfect equanimity, to perfect insight into the realities of life, to wisdom, to overflowing compassion. These are the celestial wings by which the bird of the earth soars beyond sorrow and suffering to ascend to regions of bliss supreme.

"We are marching ever forward
        On the Path of Right,
Truth will lead us safely onward
        Through this vale of night.
By its force indwelling
Ever us impelling
In our efforts ne'er to cease

Till we win release.
Yonder on the summit gleaming
Of Perfection's height,
See in wondrous glory beaming
Blest Nirvāna's light,
Steadfastly ascending,
We, our journey ending,
Shall in triumph enter in
Endless bliss to win."

19
Vipassanā Course And Code Of Discipline*

For learning Vipassana every student is required to take a ten-day residential course under a qualified teacher. For the duration of the course, the student is expected to observe Panca-Sila, five rules of moral conduct. He is to abstain from killing any sentient being, stealing, sexual misconduct (complete celibacy is to be observed during the course), telling lies and taking any intoxicants. As a student, keen on attaining complete purification of his mind, has to start with a certain degree of purity, observance of Sila is a pre-requisite, an indispensable condition for the practice of Vipassana.

To begin with, the student starts the practice by observing respiration-the flow of incoming breath and outgoing breath; just breath. By practising 'Anapana', the mind gets concentrated on the process of respiration and the student becomes aware of the relationship between mental states and respiration. As he proceeds on this path, his awareness becomes sharper, and he starts observing bodily sensations in all parts of his body. In due course, by sustained practice, one's mind gets cleaner and pure, unburdened of defilements. Awareness gets established and analytical faculty of the mind becomes sharper. There is no more sloth; there is energy. As a result, a kind of happiness descends on the mind resulting in bliss, tranquility and concentration, and finally in equantimity. These

---

* Vipassana International Academy, Dhammagiri, Igatpuri.

factors of enlightenment lead to liberation, release from all sufferings, here and now.

CODE OF DISCIPLINE

The Precepts

All students will have to observe rigorously the following Precepts:

Abstention from killing.

Abstention from stealing.

Abstention from all sexual activities.

Abstention from telling lies.

Abstention from all intoxicants.

Old students will observe three more precepts:

Abstention from taking food after 12 noon.

Abstention from sensual amusements and bodily decorations.

Abstention from using high and luxurious beds.

Old students will observe the Sixth Precept by taking only lemon water at the 5 pm break, whereas the new students will take milk or tea and fruits. The Teacher may excuse an old student from observing this precept for health reasons.

Rites, Rituals and other Techniques

For the period of the course it is absolutely essential that all rites and rituals, such as burning incense and lamps, counting beads, reciting mantras, singing and dancing, total fasting, praying etc. be totally suspended. All other meditation practices should also be suspended without condemning them. This is enjoined for the reason that the students may be able to give a fair trial to the Vipassana technique in its pristine purity and he may ensure his own protection. Students are strongly warned against mixing any type of practice with Vipassana.

Yoga and Physical Exercise

Yoga and other exercises should also be suspended. Students may exercise by walking in the areas set aside for this purpose.

Noble Silence

Students must observe Noble Silence from the start of the course until 10.00 a.m. on Day 10. Noble Silence is silence of body, speech and mind. Any form of communication, whether by physical gestures, written notes, sign language, etc., is prohibited. However, the student may speak to the Teacher whenever necessary. He may also contact the Management with any problems concerning accommodation, food, etc. All these contacts should be kept to the minimum.

Couples

Compete segregation of the sexes must be observed within the Vipassana Centre.

Talismans, rosaries, sacred threads etc.

All such items should not be brought to the Centre, If they are brought inadvertently, they should be deposited with the Management for the duration of the course.

Smoking

Smoking or chewing tobacco is not allowed inside the Centre.

Clothing

There should be modesty and decorum in dress at the Centre suited to the serious nature of the work. Transparent or revealing dresses are not allowed.

Outside Contacts

Students will have to remain inside the Centre FOR THE ENTIRE COURSE. They may leave only with the specific consent of the Teacher. All telephone calls, letters and contacts with visitors will have to be suspended. In any emergency a visitor may contact the Management. Students are also requested not to communicate with the Centre's staff (except the Management).

Food

It is not possible to satisfy the special food requirements of all the meditators from so many different countries and cultures. The students are therefore kindly requested to make do with the simple Indian vegetarian menu provided.

Reading and Writing

No writing or reading materials, including religious works and even books on Vipassana, should be brought into the Centre. New students should not distract themselves by taking notes. The restriction on reading and writing is to emphasise the strictly practical nature of this meditation.

Cost of Boarding and Lodging

There is absolutely no fee for the Dhamma Teaching. The cost of boarding and lodging is met by donations of the old students.

No donation is accepted from a new student on his joining the course. However, at the end of the course he is welcome to express his feeling of satisfaction and goodwill by offering donations in keeping with his volition.

The Time Table

The following time table has been designed to maintain the continuity of practice. Students are advised to follow it as closely as possible for best results.

4.00 a.m.	Morning wake up bell
4.30-6.30	Meditation in hall or residence
6.30-8.00	Breakfast break
8.00-9.00	Group Meditation in hall
9.00-11.00	Meditation in hall or residence, as per instructions of the Teacher.

11.00-12.00	Lunch
12.00-1.00	Rest
1.00-2.30	Meditation in hall or residence
2.30-3.30	Group Meditation in hall
3.30-5.00	Meditation in hall or residence, as per instructions of the Teacher.
5.00-6.00	Tea break
6.00-7.00	Group meditation in hall
7.00-8.30	Teacher's discourse in hall
8.30-9.00	Group Meditation in hall
9.00-9.30	Question time in hall
9.30 pm	Retire to own room, Lights out.

Notwithstanding the rigid rules and regulations, the code of conduct, and the time table, the Vipassana is becoming popular rapidly in India and abroad. The Vipassana Light which originated from the Dhammagiri at Igatpuri in Maharashtra has since engulfed the whole world.

20
Satipaṭṭhāna Sutta*

Ven. Nyanasatta Thera

Thus have I heard. At one time the Blessed One was living among the Kurus, at Kammāsadamma a market town of the Kuru people. There the Blessed One addressed the bhikkhus thus: 'Monks', and they replied to him. 'Venerable Sir.' The Blessed One spoke as follows:

This is the only way, monks for the purification of beings, for the overcoming of soorow and lamentation, for the destruction of suffering and grief, for reaching the right path, for the attainment of Nibbāna, namely the Four Foundations of Mindfulness. What are the four?

Herein (in this teaching) a monk lives contemplating the body in the body,[1] ardent, clearly comprehending and mindful, having overcome, in this world, covetousness and grief; he lives contemplating feeling in feelings, ardent, clearly comprehending and mindful, having overcome, in this world, covetousness and grief; he lives contemplating consciousness in consciousness,[2] ardent, clearly comprehending and mindful, having overcome, in this world, covetousness and grief; he lives contemplating mental objects in mental objects.[2] ardent, clearly comprehending and mindful, having overcome, in this world, covetousness and grief.

---

* Buddhist Publication Society, Kandy, Sri Lanka, Wheel Publication No. 19.

I. The Contemplation of the Body

1. Mindfulness of Breathing

And how does a monk live contemplating the body in the body?

Herein, monks, a monk having gone to the forest, to the foot of a tree or to an empty place, sits down, with his legs crossed, keeps his body erect and his mindfulness alert.[3]

Ever mindful he breathes in, and mindful he breathes out. Breathing in a long breath, he knows 'I am breathing in a long breath'; breathing out a long breath, he knows 'I am breathing out a long breath'; breathing in a short breath, he knows 'I am breathing in a short breath'; breathing out a short breath, he knows 'I am breathing out a short breath.'

'Experiencing the whole (breath-) body, I shall breathe in', thus he trains himself. 'Experiencing the whole (breath-) body, I shall breathe out', thus he trains himself. 'Calming the activity of the (breath-) body, I shall breathe in', thus he trains himself. 'Calming the activity of the (breath-) body. I shall breathe out', thus he trains himself.

Just as a skillful turner or turner's apprentice, making a long turn, knows 'I am making a long turn', or making a short turn, knows, 'I am making a short turn, just so the monk, breathing in a long breath, knows 'I am breathing in a long breath'; breathing out a long breath, knows 'I am breathing out a long breath'; breathing in a short breath, knows 'I am breathing in a short breath'; breathing out a short breath, knows 'I am breathing out a short breath'. 'Experiencing the whole (breath-) body, I shall breathe in', thus he trains himself'. 'Experiencing the whole (breath-) body, I shall breathe out', thus he trains himself. 'Calming the activity of the (breath-) body, I shall breathe in', thus he trains himself. 'Calming the activity of the (breath-) body. I shall breathe out', thus he trains himself.

Thus he lives contemplating the body in the body internally, or he lives contemplating the body in the body externally, or he

lives contemplating the body in the body, internally and externally.[4]
He lives contemplating origination-factors[5] in the body, or he lives
contemplating dissolution factors[6] in the body, or he lives
contemplating origination-and-dissolution factors[7] in the body. Or
his mindfulness is established with the thought: The body exists'[8]
to the extent necessary just for knowledge and mindfulness, and he
lives independent,[9] and clings to naught in the world. Thus also
monks, a monk lives contemplating the body in the body.

2. The Postures of the Body

And further, monks, a monk knows when he is going 'I am
going': he knows when he is standing 'I am standing'; he knows
when he is sitting 'I am sitting'; he knows when he is lying down
'I am lying down'; or just as his body is disposed so he knows it.

Thus he lives contemplating the body in the body internally,
or he lives contemplating the body in the body externally, or he
lives contemplating the body in the body internally and externally.
He lives contemplating origination-factors in the body, or he lives
contemplating dissolution-factors in the body, or he lives
contemplating origination-and-dissolution factors in the body.[10] or
his mindfulness is established with the thought: 'The body exists',
to the extent necessary just for knowledge and mindfulness, and he
lives independent, and clings to naught in the world. Thus also,
monks, a monk lives contemplating the body in the body.

3. Mindfulness with Clear Comprehension

And further, monks, a monk, in going forward and back,
applies clear comprehension; in looking straight on and looking
away, he applies clear comprehension; in bending and in stretching,
he applies clear comprehension; in wearing robes and carrying the
bowl, he applies clear comprehension; in eating, drinking, chewing
and savouring, he applies clear comprehension; in attending to the
calls of nature, he applies clear comprehension; in walking, in
standing, in sitting, in falling asleep, in waking, in speaking and in
keeping silence, he applies clear comprehension.

Thus he lives contemplating the body in the body...

4. The Reflection on the Repulsiveness of the Body

And further, monks, a monk reflects on this very body enveloped by the skin and full of manifold impurity, from the sole up, and from the top of the head hair down, thinking thus: "There are in this body hair of the head, hair of the body, nails, teeth, skin, flesh, sinews, bones, marrow, kidney, heart, liver, midriff, spleen, lungs, intestines, mesentery, gorge, faeces, bile, phlegm, pus, blood, sweat, fat, tears, grease, saliva, nasal mucus, synovial fluid, urine'.

Just as if there were a doubled-mouthed provision bag full of various kinds of grain such as hill paddy, paddy, green gram, cow-peas, sesamum, and husked rice, and a man with sound eyes, having opened that bag, were to take stock of the contents thus:—This is hill paddy, this is paddy, this is green gram, this is cow-peas, this is sesamum, this is husked rice. Just so, monks, a monk reflects on this very body enveloped by the skin and full of manifold impurity, from the soles up and from the top of the head hair down, thinking thus: There are in this body hair of the head, hair of the body, nails, teeth, skin, flesh, sinews, bones, marrow, kidney, heart, liver, midriff, spleen, lungs, intestines, mesentery, gorge, faeces, bile, phlegm, pus, blood, sweat, fat, tears, grease, saliva, nasal mucus, synovial fluid, urine.

Thus he lives contemplating the body in the body...

5. The Reflection on the Material Elements

And further, monks, a monk reflects on this very body however it be placed or disposed, by way of the material elements: "There are in this body the element of earth, the element of water, the element of fire, the element of wind.[11]

Just as if, monks, a clever cow-butcher or his apprentice, having slaughtered a cow and divided it into portions, should be sitting at the junction of four high roads, in the same way, a monk reflects on this very body, as it is placed or disposed, by way of the material elements: "There are in this body the elements of earth, water, fire and wind'.

Thus he lives contemplating the body in the body...

6. The Nine Cemetery Contemplations

(1) And further, monks, as if a monk sees a body dead one, two, or three days; swollen, blue and festering, thrown in the charnel ground, he then applies this perception to his own body thus: 'Verily, also my own body is of the same nature; such it will become and will not escape it'.

Thus he lives contemplating the body in the body internally, or lives contemplating the body in the body externally, or lives contemplating the body in the body internally and externally. He lives contemplating dissolution-factors in the body, or he lives contemplating origination-and-dissolution-factors in the body. Or his mindfulness is established with the thought: 'The body exists', to the extent necessary just for knowledge and mindfulness, and he lives independent, and clings to naught in the world. Thus also, monks, a monk lives contemplating the body in the body.

(2) And further, monks, as if a monk sees a body thrown in the charnel ground, being eaten by crows, hawks, vultures, dogs, jackals or by different kinds of worms, he then applies this perception to his own body thus: 'Verily, also my own body is of the same nature; such it will become and will not escape it.

Thus he lives contemplating the body in the body. . .

(3) And further, monks, as if a monk sees a body thrown in the charnel ground and reduced to a skeleton with some flesh and blood attached to it, held together by the tendons. . .

(4) And further, monks, as if a monk sees a body thrown in the charnel ground and reduced to a skeleton, blood-be-smeared and without flesh, held together by the tendons. . .

(5) And further, monks, as if a monk sees a body thrown in the charnel ground and reduced to a skeleton without flesh and blood, held togehter by the tendons. . .

(6) And further, monks, as if a monk sees a body thrown in the charnel ground and reduced to disconnected bones, scattered in all directions—here a bone of the hand, there a bone of the foot, a shin bone, a thigh bone, the pelvis, spine and skull. . .

(7) And further, monks, as if a monk sees a body thrown in the charnel ground, reduced to bleached bones of conch-like colour...

(8) And further, monks, as if a monk sees a body thrown in the charnel ground, reduced to bones, more than a year old, lying in a heap...

(9) And further, monks, as if a monk sees a body thrown in the charnel ground, reduced to bones gone rotten and become dust.

He then applies this perception to his own body thus: 'Verily, also my own body is of the same nature; such it will become and will not escape it'.

Thus he lives contemplating the body in the body internally, or he lives contemplating the body in the body externally, or he lives contemplating the body in the body internally and externally. He lives contemplating origination-factors in the body, or he lives contemplating dissolution-factors in the body, or he lives contemplating origination-and-dissolution-factors in the body. Or his mindfulness is established with the thought : 'The body exists', to the extent necessary just for knowledge and mindfulness, and he lives independent, and clings to naught in the world. Thus also, monks, a monk lives contemplating the body in the body.

II. The Contemplation of Feeling

And how, monks, does a monk live contemplating feelings in feelings?

Herein, monks, a monk when experiencing a pleasant feeling knows, 'I experience a pleasant feeling'; when experiencing a painful feeling, he knows, 'I experience a painful feeling'; when experiencing a neither-pleasant-nor-painful feeling', he knows, 'I experience a neither-pleasant-nor-painful feeling'. When experiencing a pleasant worldly feeling, he knows, 'I experience a pleasant worldly feeling': when experiencing a pleasant spiritual feeling, he knows, 'I experience a pleasant spiritual feeling'; when experiencing a painful worldly feeling, he knows, 'I experience a painful worldly feeling'; when experiencing a painful spiritual feeling, he knows. 'I experience a pleasant spiritual feeling'; when experiencing a painful worldly feeling, he knows, 'I experience a painful worldly feeling'; when experiencing a painful spiritual feeling': when experiencing a neither-pleasant-nor-painful worldly feeling, he knows. 'I experience a neither-pleasant-nor-painful worldly feeling'; when experiencing a neither-pleasant-nor-painful spiritual feeling, he knows, 'I experience a neither-pleasant-nor-painful spiritual feeling'.

Thus he lives contemplating feelings in feelings internally, or he lives contemplating feelings in feelings internally and externally. He lives contemplating origination-factors in feelings, or he lives contemplating dissolution-factors in feelings, or he lives contemplating origination-and-dissolution factors in feelings.[12] Or his mindfulness is established with the thought, 'Feeling exists', to the extent necessary just for knowledge and mindfulness, and he lives independent, and clings to naught in the world. Thus, monks, a monk lives contemplating feelings in feelings.

III. The Contemplation of Consciousness

And how, monks, does a monk live contemplating consciousness in consciousness?

Herein, monks, a monk knows the consciousness with lust, as with lust; the consciousness without lust, as without lust; the consciousness with hate, as with hate; the consciousness without hate, as without hate; the consciousness with ignorance, as with ignorance; the consciousness without ignorance, as without ignorance; the shrunken state of consciousness as the shrunken state;[13] the distracted state of consciousness as the distracted state;[14] the developed state of consciousness as the developed state;[15] the undeveloped state of consciousness as the undeveloped state;[16] the state of consciousness with some other mental state superior to it, as the state with something mentally higher;[17] the state of consciousness with no other mental state superior to it, as the state with nothing mentally higher;[18] the concentrated state of consciousness as the concentrated state; the unconcentrated state of consciusness as the unconcentrated state; the freed state of consciousness as the freed state;[19] and the unfreed state of conscious as the unfreed.

Thus he lives contemplting consciousness in consciousness internally, or he lives contemplating consciousness in consciousness externally, or he lives contemplating consciousness in consciousness internally and externally. He lives contemplating origination-factors in consciousness, or he lives contemplating dissloution-factors in consciousness, or he lives contemplating origination-and-dissolution-factors in consciousness.[20] Or his mindfulness is established with the thought, 'Consciousness exist', to the extent necessary just for knowledge and mindfulness, and he lives independent, and clings to naught in the world. Thus, monks lives contemplating consciousness in consciousness.

IV. The Contemplation of Mental Objects

1. The Five Hindrances

And how, monks, does a monk live contemplating mental objects in mental objects?

Herein, monks, a monk lives contemplating mental objects in the mental objects of the five hindrances.

How, monks, does a monk live contemplating mental objects in the mental objects of the five hindrances?

Herein, monks, when *sense-desire* is present, a monk knows, "There is sense-desire in me', or when sense-desire is not present, he knows, "There is no sense-desire in me'. He knows how the arising of the non-arisen sense-desire comes to be; he knows how the abandoning of the arisen sense-desire comes to be; and he knows how the non-arising in the future of the abandoned sense-desire comes to be.

When *anger* is present, he knows, 'There is anger in me', or when anger is not present, he knows, 'There is no anger in me'. He knows how the arising of the non-arisen anger comes to be; he knows how the abandoning of the arisen anger comes to be; and he knows how the non-arising in the future of the abandoned anger comes to be.

When *sloth and torpor* are present, he knows, 'There are sloth and torpor in me', or when sloth and torpor are not present, he knows, 'There are no sloth and torpor in me'. He knows how the arising of the non-arisen sloth and torpor comes to be; he knows how the abandoning of the arisen sloth and torpor comes to be; and he knows how the non-arising in the future of the abandoned sloth and torpor comes to be.

When *agitation* and *scruples* are present, he knows, 'There are agitation and scruples in me' or when agitation and scruples are not present, he knows, 'There are no agitation and scruples in me'. He knows how the arising of the non-arisen agitation and scruples comes to be; he know how the abandoning of the arisen agitation and scruples comes to be; and he knows how the non-arising in the future of the abandoned agitation and scruples comes to be.

When *doubt* is present, he knows, "There is doubt in me', or when doubt is not present, he knows, 'There is no doubt in me'. He knows how the arising of the non-arisen doubt comes to be; he knows how the abandoning of the arisen doubt comes to be; and he knows how the non-arising in the future of the abandoned doubt comes to be.

Thus he lives contemplating mental objects in mental objects internally, or he lives contemplating mental objects in mental objects externally, or he lives contemplating mental objects in mental objects internally and externally. He lives contemplating origination-factors in mental objects, or he lives contemplating dissolution-factors in mental objects, or he lives contemplating origination-and-dissolution-factors in mental objects.[21] Or his mindfulness is established with the thought, 'Mental objects exist', to the extent necessary just for knowledge and mindfulness, and he lives independent, and clings to naught in the world. Thus also, monks, a monk lives contemplating mental objects in the mental objects of the five hindrances.

2. The Five Aggregates of Clinging

And further, monks, a monk lives contemplating mental objects in the mental objects of the five aggregates of clinging.[22]

How, monks, does a monk live contemplating mental objects in the mental objects of the five aggregates of clinging?

Herein, monks, a monk thinks, 'Thus is *material form;* thus is the arising of material form; and thus is the disappearance of material form. Thus is *feeling;* thus is the arising of feeling; and thus is the disappearance of feeling. Thus is *perception;* thus is the disappearance of feeling. Thus is *perception;* thus is the arising of perception; and thus is the disappearance of perception. Thus are *formations;* Thus is the arising of formations; and thus is the disappearance of formations. Thus is *consciousness;* thus is the arising of consciousness; and thus is the disappearance of consciousness'.

Thus he lives contemplating mental objects in mental objects internally, or he lives contemplating mental objects externally, or he lives contemplating mental objects in mental objects internally and externally. He lives contemplaging origination-factors in mental objects, or he lives contemplating dissolution-factors in mental objects, or he lives contemplating origination-and-dissolution-factors in mental objects.[23] Or his mindfulness is established with the thought, 'mental objects exist', to the extent necessary just for knowledge and mindfulness, and he lives independent, and clings to naught in the world. Thus also, monks, a monk lives contemplating mental objects in the mental objects of the five aggregates of clinging.

3. The Six Internal and the Six External Sense-Bases

And further, monks, a monk lives contemplating mental objects in the mental objects of the six internal and the six external sense-bases.

How, monks, does a monk live contemplating mental objects in the mental objects of the six internal and the six external sense-bases?

Herein, monks, a monk knows, *the eye and visual forms,* and the fetter that arises dependent on both (the eye and forms);[24] he knows how the arising of the non-arisen fetter comes to be, he knows how the abandoning of the arisen fetter comes to be; and he knows how the non-arising in the future of the abandoned fetter comes to be.

He knows the *ear* and *sounds*...the *nose* and *smells*...the *tongue* and *flavours*...the *body* and *tactual objects*...the *mind* and *mental objects,* and the fetter that arises dependent on both; he knows how the arising of the non-arisen fetter comes to be; he knows how the abandoning of the arisen fetter comes to be; and he knows how the non-arising in the future of the abandoned fetter comes to be.

Thus, monk, the monk lives contemplating mental objects in mental objects internally, or he lives contemplating mental objects in mental objects externally, or he lives contemplating mental objects in mental objects internally and externally. He lives contemplating origination-factors in mental objects, or he lives contemplating dissolution-factors in mental objects, or he lives contemplating origination-and-dissolution-factors in mental objects.[25] Or his mindfulness is established with the thought, 'Mental objects exist', to the extent necessary just for knowledge and mindfulness, and he lives independent, and clings to naught in the world. Thus, monks, a monk lives contemplating mental objects in the mental objects of the six internal and the six external sense-bases.

4. The Seven Factors of Enlightenment

And further, monks, a monk lives contemplating mental objects in the mental objects of the seven factors of enlightenment.

How, monks, does a monk live contemplating mental objects in the mental objects of the seven factors of enlightenment.

Herein, monks, when the enlightenment-factor of *mindfulness* is present, the monk knows, 'The enlightenment-factor of mindfulness is in me'; or when the enlightenment-factor of mindfulness is absent, he knows. The enlightenment-factor of mindfulness is not in me'; and he knows how the arising of the

non-arisen enlightenment-factor of mindfulness comes to be; and
how perfection in the development of the arisen enlightenment-factor
of mindfulness comes to be.

When the enlightenment-factor of *the investigation of mental
objects* is present, the monk knows 'The enlightenment-factor of
the investigation of mental objects is in me'; when the enlightenment-
factor of the investigation of mental objects is absent, he knows.
'enlightenment-factor of the investigation of mental objects is not
in me'; and he knows how the arising of the non-arisen
enlightenment-factor of the investigation of mental objects comes
to be, and how perfection in the development of the arisen
enlightenment-factor of the mindfulness comes to be.

When the enlightenment-factor of *energy* is present, he knows,
'The enlightement-factor of energy is in me'; when the
enlightenment-factor of energy is absent, he knows, 'The
enlightenment-factor of energy is not in me'; and he knows how
the arising of the non-arisen enlightenment-factor of energy comes
to be, and how perfection in the development of the arisen
enlightenment-factor of energy comes to be.

When the enlightenment-factor of *joy* is present, he knows,
'The enlightenment-factor of joy is in me'; when the enlightenment-
factor of joy is absent he knows, "The enlightenment-factor of joy
is not in me'; and he knows how the arising of the non-arisen
enlightenment-factor of joy comes to be, and how perfection in the
development of the arisen enlightenment-factor of joy comes to be.

When the enlightenment-factor of *tranquillity* is present, he
knows. The enlightenment-factor of tranquillity is in me'; when
the enlightenment-factor of tranquillity is absent, he knows, "The
enlightenment-factor of tranquillity is not in me'; and he knows the
arising of the non-arisen enlightenment-factor of tranquillity comes
to be, and how perfection in the development of the arisen
enlightenment-factor of tranqillity comes to be.

When the enlightenment-factor of *concentration* is present,
he knows. "The enlightenment-factor of concentration is in me';
when the enlightenment-factor of concentration is absent, he knows,
'The enlightenment-factor of concentration is not in me'; and he

knows how the arising of the non-arisen enlightenment-factor of concentraton comes to be, and how perfection in the development of the arisen enlightenment-factor of concentration comes to be. When the enlightenment-factor of *equanimity* is present, he knows, 'The enlightenment-factor of equanimity is in me'; when the enlightenment-factor of equanimity is absent, he knows, "The enlightenment-factor of equanimity is not in me'; and he knows how the arising of the non-arisen enlightenment-factor of equanimity comes to be, and how perfection in the development of the arisen enlightenment-factor of equanimity comes to be.

Thus he lives contemplating mental objects in mental objects internally, or he lives contemplating mental objects in mental objects externally, or he lives contemplating mental objects in mental objects internally and externally. He lives contemplating origination-factors in mental objects, or he lives contemplating dissolution-factors in mental objects, or he lives contemplating origination-and-dissolution-factors in mental objects.[26] Or his mindfulness is established with the thought, 'Mental objects exist', to the extent necessary just for knowledge and mindfulness, and he lives independent, and clings to naught in the world. Thus, monks, a monk lives contemplating mental objects in the mental objects of the seven factors of enlightenment.

5. The Four Noble Truths

And further, monks, a monk lives contemplating mental objects in the mental objects of the four noble truths.

How, monks, does a monk live contemplating mental objects in the mental objects of the four noble truths?

Herein, monks, a monk knows, '*This is suffering*', according to reality; he knows, '*This is the origin of suffering*', according to reality; he knows, '*This is the cessation of suffering*', according to reality; he knows, '*This is the road leading to the cessation of suffering*', according to reality.

Thus he lives contemplating mental objects in mental objects internally, or he lives contemplating mental objects in mental objects externally, or he lives contemplating mental objects in mental objects internally and externally. He lives contemplating origination-factors in mental objects, or he lives contemplating dissolution-factors in mental objects, or he lives contemplating origination-and-dissolution-factors in mental objects.[27] Or his mindfulness is established with the thought, 'Mental objects exist', to the extent necessary just for knowledge and mindfulness, and he lives independent, and clings to naught in the world. Thus, monks, a monk lives contemplating mental objects in the mental objects of the four noble truths.

Verily, monks, whosoever practises these four Foundations of Mindfulness in this manner for seven years, then one of these two fruits may be expected by him: Highest Knowledge (Arahantship), here and now, or if some remainder of clinging is yet present, the state of Non-returning.[28]

O monks, let alone seven years. Should any person practise these four Foundations of Mindfulness in this manner for six years...for five years...four years...three years...two years...one year, then one of these two fruits may be expected by him: Highest Knowledge, here and now, or if some remainder of clinging is yet present, the state of Non-returning.

O monks, let alone a year. Should any person practise these four Foundations of Mindfulness in this manner for seven months...for six months...five months...four months...three months...two months...a month...half a month, then one of these two fruits may be expected by him: Hightest Knowledge, here and now, or if some remainder of clinging is yet present, the state of Non-returning.

O monks, let alone half a month. Should any person practise these four Foundations of Mindfulness, in this manner, for a week, then one of these two fruits may be expected by him: Highest Knowledge, here and now, or if some remainder of clinging is yet present, the state of Non-returning.

Because of this was it said: 'This is the only way, monks, for the purification of beings, for the overcoming of sorrow and lamentation, for the destruction of suffering and grief, for reaching

the right path, for the attainment of Nibbāna, namely the four
Foundations of Mindfulness'.

Thus spoke the Blessed One. Satisfied the monks approved
of his words.

Satipaṭṭhāna Sutta, Majjhima Nikāya, Sutta No. 10.

References

1. The repetition of the phrases 'contemplating the body in the
    body', 'feelings in feelings', etc. is meant to impress upon the
    meditator the importance of remaining aware whether, in the
    sustained attention directed upon a single chosen object, one
    is still keeping to it, and has not strayed into the field of another
    Contemplation. For instance, when contemplating any bodily
    process, a meditator may unwittingly be side-tracked into a
    consideration of his *feelings* connected with that bodily process.
    He should then be clearly aware that he has left his original
    subject, and is engaged in the Contemplation of Feeling.

2. Mind. Pāli *citta*, also consciousness or viññāna, in this
    connection are the states of mind or units in the stream of mind
    of momentary duration. Mental objects, *dhamma*, are the mental
    contents or factors of consciousness making up the single states
    of mind.

3. Literally, 'setting up mindfulness in front'.

4. 'Internally': contemplating his own breathing; 'externally',
    contemplating another's breathing; "internally and externally";
    contemplating one's own and another's breathing, alternately,
    with uninterrupted attention. In the beginning one pays
    attention to one's own breathing only, and it is only in advanced
    stages that for the sake of practising insight, one by inference
    pays at times attention also to another person's process of
    breathing.

5. The origination-factors (*samudaya-dhammā*), that is, the
    conditions of the origination of the breath-body; these are: the
    body in its entirety, nasal aperture and mind.

6. The conditions of the dissolution of the breath-body, are: the
    destruction of the body and of the nasal aperture, and the
    ceasing of mental activity.

7. The contemplation of both, alternately.

8. That is, only impersonal bodily processes exist, without a self, soul, spirit or abiding essence or substance. The coresponding phrase in the following Contemplations should be understood accordingly.

9. Independent from craving and wrong view.

10. All contemplations of the Body, excepting the preceding one, have as factors of origination: ignorance, craving, kamma, food, and the general characteristic of originating; the factors of dissolution are: disappearance of ignorance, craving, kamma, food, and the general characteristic of dissolving.

11. The so-called 'elements' are the primary quaiities of matter, explained by Buddhist tradition as solidity (earth), adhesion (water), caloricity (fire) and motion (wind or air).

12. The factors of origination are here : ignorance, craving, kamma, and sense-impression, and the general characteristic of originating; the factors of dissolution are: the disappearance of the four, and the general characteristic of dissolving.

13. This refers to a rigid and indolent state of mind.

14. This refers to a restless mind.

15. The consciousness of the meditative Absorptions of the fine-corporeal and uncorporeal sphere (rūpa-arūpa-jhāna).

16. The ordinary consciousness of the sensuous state of existence (kāmāvacara).

17. The consciousness of the sensuous state of existence, having other mental states superior to it.

18. The consciousness of the fine-corporeal and the uncorporeal spheres, having no mundane mental state superior to it.

19. Temporarily freed from the defilements either through the methodical practice of Insight (vipassanā) freeing from single evil states by force of their opposites, or through the meditative Absorptions (jhāna).

20. The factors of origination consist here of ignorance, craving, kamma, body-and-mind (nāma-rūpa), and of the general characteristic of originating; the factors of dissolution are: the disappearance of ignorance, etc., and the general characteristic of dissolving.

21. The factors of origination are here the conditions which produce the Hindrances, as wrong reflection, etc.; the factors of dissolution are the conditions which remove the Hindrances, e.g. right reflection.

22. These five groups or aggregates constitute the so-called personality. By making them objects of clinging, existence, in form of repeated births and deaths, is perpetuated.

23. The origination-and-dissolution-factors of the five Aggregates: for Material Form, the same as for the Postures (Note 10); for Feeling, the same as for the Contemplation of Feeling (Note 12); for Perception and Formations, the same as for Feeling (Note 12); for Consciousness, the same as for the Contemplation of Consciousness (Note 20).

24. The usual enumeration of the ten principal Fetters (*samyojanā*), as given in the Discourse Collection (Sutta Pitaka), is as follows: 1. self-illusion, 2. scepticism, 3. attachment to rules and rituals, 4. sensual lust, 5. ill-will, 6. craving for fine-corporeal existence, 7. craving for uncorporeal existence, 8. conceit, 9. restlessness, 10. ignorance.

25. Origination-factors of the ten physical sense-bases are ignorance, craving, kamma, food, and the general characteristic of originating; dissolution-factors: the general characteristic of dissolving and the disappearance of ignorance, etc. The origination-and-dissolution-factors of the mind-base are the same as those of feeling (Note 12).

26. Just the conditions conducive to the origination and dissolution of the Factors of Enlightenment comprise the origination-and-dissolution-factors here.

27. The origination-and-dissolution factors of the Truths should be understood as the arising and passing of Suffering, Craving, and the Path; the Truth of Cessation is not to be included in this contemplation since it has neither origination nor dissolution.

28. That is the non-returning to the world of sensuality. This is the last stage before the attainment of the final goal of Saintship, or Arahatship.

INDEX